INTERNET RESEARCH METHODS:
A Practical Guide for the Social and Behavioural Sciences

Claire Hewson
Peter Yule
Dianna Laurent
Carl Vogel

SAGE Publications
London • Thousand Oaks • New Delhi

© Hewson, Yule, Laurent, Vogel 2003

First Published 2003
Reprinted 2003

 SAGE Publications Ltd
6 Bonhill Street
London EC2A 4PU

SAGE Publications Inc
2455 Teller Road
Thousand Oaks, California 91320

SAGE Publications India Pvt Ltd
32, M-Block Market
Greater Kailash - I
New Delhi 110 048

British Library Cataloguing in Publication data

A catalogue record for this book is
available from the British Library

ISBN 0 7619 5919 X
ISBN 0 7619 5920 3 (pbk)

Library of Congress Control Number: 2002101992

Typeset by Photoprint, Torquay, Devon, UK
Printed in Great Britain by Athenaeum Press, Gateshead

Contents

Acknowledgements

We would like to thank the editorial staff at Sage for all their support and help in bringing *Internet Research Methods* to completion. We are especially thankful to Ray Lee and Nigel Fielding for their helpful suggestions.

List of Figures

List of Abbreviations

1

Introduction

This book provides a comprehensive guide to conducting research on the Internet. We distinguish between what we term *primary* and *secondary* research: the former refers to research that gathers data from participants; the latter to research that utilises secondary information sources (such as books and journal articles). In an Internet context, primary research is that which makes use of the Internet to recruit participants, administer materials, and collect responses. Secondary research concerns the use of the Internet to access information available online, from resources such as library databases and online journals. These descriptions of primary and secondary Internet research are approximate: for example, we would consider linguistic observation studies that make use of logs of Internet-based communications (for example, archived chat room discussion, or newsgroup postings) to be primary research. Similarly, we would classify a discourse analysis of archived online material as primary research. Essentially, any approach that involves analysis of data to produce novel evidence we would consider primary research.

Active researchers and students alike may find the Internet useful for both primary and secondary research. Thus we have aimed to make the book accessible to both. In relation to secondary research, the book outlines a range of the most useful resources available for social and behavioural research, and explains how to use these effectively. Using the Internet to locate secondary resources can have great pedagogical value and, we argue, enhance (but not replace) more traditional library-based methods. For those involved in research and teaching, the wealth of information available online – from databases of journal articles, to copies of lecture notes – is invaluable. These resources can help locate information quickly and cost-effectively. The important issue to bear in mind is establishing the quality and accuracy of the resources found, and the book provides guidelines for ensuring this.

Use of the Internet as a primary research tool is discussed extensively in this book. Interest in this usage of the Internet is clearly developing, as more and more studies appear online, as well as an increasing body of literature emerging on the topic. Yet, at the time of writing, many issues are just starting to be addressed. The book highlights and explores these issues, many of which require further research before effective solutions can be offered. However, based on our own experiences, we are able to present a preliminary set of guidelines and recommendations, as well as highlight areas that need further research. The experience we draw upon includes our own use of the Internet as a research tool. All of the authors involved in writing this book have used the Internet as a primary and/or secondary research tool. We have gathered data via the Internet to address research questions in our areas of interest, which include human reasoning and common-sense psychology. We have reviewed the Internet-mediated research (IMR) literature, piloted software procedures, and developed IMR guidelines and recommendations. Presently, we are engaged in further development of software procedures, as well as research that aims to clarify the influence of various factors in IMR, and to validate IMR procedures. This experience is drawn upon in discussions throughout the book.

IMR may benefit students who are undertaking an undergraduate project, or conducting postgraduate research, due to the scope for obtaining large volumes of data in a short time and with minimal costs. Researchers at smaller institutions, where the resources available (time and funding) for supporting research may be more limited, may similarly benefit. The book provides enough information to allow the reader to design and implement an Internet-based study.

The disciplinary scope of the book is intended to be broad. We have aimed to present information that is relevant to research across a range of disciplines that fall within the general category of the social and behavioural sciences.[1] Indeed, the diversity of methodologies discussed (which includes questionnaires, interviews, observational studies, and experiments) are used across a broad range of disciplines. No doubt, certain disciplines, or sub-areas within those disciplines, will tend to favour one or other methodology (for example, psychological research has been closely associated with the experimental design), but the information presented should be broad enough in scope for researchers from different disciplines to pick out what is relevant to their own particular research domain. This is not to suggest that the book does not also deliver detailed information on how to implement specific methodologies (indeed the book includes illustrations, case studies, and detailed discussion of software procedures and programming code), but simply that it is not restricted to a consideration of any one discipline or research area. Having noted this, the majority of illustrations we use do refer to work within psychology and cognitive science, since these are the disciplines we work within (and many of these examples are drawn from our own research). We hope that researchers from other disciplines will not find this off-putting, and will be inspired to apply the general principles and procedures outlined to specific issues within their own discipline.

An important aspect of the book is that it does not assume any prior computing expertise, at least not beyond some basic skills such as sending and receiving emails, and reading and posting to newsgroups.[2] Thus the book is aimed at providing the practising researcher, or student, who has some minimal level of computer-literacy, with the necessary information, tools, and insights to be able to assess the extent to which the Internet can help support his or her research needs, and to be able to carry out Internet-based research. For secondary research, detailed procedures for accessing the materials described are given. For primary research, we supplement our discussion of the tools and procedures available with illustrative examples and case studies. We take care to include methodologies that demonstrate how IMR can be carried out with minimal technical expertise. However, we also spend some considerable time looking at more complex procedures that do require fairly sophisticated programs and implementation systems, since these offer the most scope for addressing a wide range of research designs. While the interested reader may attend to the computing details offered (Chapter 5), it is not necessary to learn how to program to get an Internet study up and running. This is because there are a range of packages currently being developed that are aimed precisely at allowing the researcher who is not interested in becoming a programming expert to design and implement a Web-based study.[3] The book refers to several such packages already available for use, though at the time of writing none of these have undergone rigorous development and testing. Nevertheless they are useful. Although an aim of the book is accessibility to the non-computer expert, some familiarity with computer- and Internet-related terminology is required. However, the approach has been to fully explain these terms as far as possible.

In addition to providing information on the 'nuts and bolts' of Internet-mediated research, an important aspect of this book is a consideration of the theoretical, methodological, and ethical issues that IMR raises. Sampling bias and the Internet-user population is one such issue. Respecting privacy in IMR is another. These issues are highlighted and discussed early on in the book, and then taken up in more detail in later chapters, which outline how the issues interact with specific procedures and implementations. The scope for IMR is also discussed early on, through consideration of the range of methodologies that can be adapted to an Internet-mediated approach, and the advantages and disadvantages of using IMR as opposed to more traditional approaches. Details of the tools and procedures available to support these methodologies are then discussed. Emphasis is placed upon providing guidelines and

recommendations that will allow the researcher to implement procedures that maximise the validity of his or her data. Potential problems are
also highlighted so that the researcher may be forewarned of these, and
take steps to avoid them. In the unfortunate event that problems do
occur (even in a carefully designed study unforeseen problems can
nevertheless arise), recovery strategies are suggested.

Thus the book is aimed at the practising researcher who is not an
expert programmer but who is interested in using the Internet as a tool
for enhancing and expanding his or her own research. We now give a
brief outline of the history of the Internet, followed by a description of
the content of each chapter.

History of the Internet

Internet grew out of the ARPANET (Advanced Research Projects Agency
Network), commissioned in 1969 by the US Department of Defense for
research into computer networking (for a more detailed history of
Internet, see Zakon, 2000). In 1971 there were 15 nodes on ARPANET
connecting 23 host computers. Email was invented in 1972 by Ray
Tomlinson of Bolt Beranek and Newman (BBN). The first international
connections did not come until 1973, when the UK and Norway each
added nodes. BBN introduced the first commercial version of ARPANET
in 1974. From then a number of network systems emerged, including
USENET in 1979 and BITNET in 1981. The latter started as a cooperative
email based system between the City University of New York and Yale.
The first MUD (Multi-User Dungeon) was produced in 1979 by Bartle
and Trubshaw of the University of Essex. Protocols, Transmission Control Protocol (TCP) and Internet Protocol (IP) were introduced in 1982.

Effectively, 'Internet' began with that standardisation and denotes
networked TCP/IP systems. It was not until 1984 that the number of
networked host computers exceeded 1,000, and in that same year the
Japan UNIX Network was put into place, as was the Joint Academic
Network (JANET) in the United Kingdom. In 1986 the NSFNET
(National Science Foundation Network) was established by NASA and
the US Department of Energy as a way to facilitate connections outside
the ARPANET security and bureaucracy. By 1987 the number of Internet
hosts exceeded 10,000, and BITNET hit the 1,000 point. Just a year later
there were 60,000 Internet hosts, this number increasing to over 100,000
within the next year. By 1992 the number of Internet hosts stood at over
1,000,000, increasing to 3.2 million by July 1994, and reaching a figure of
56,218 million networked hosts by July 1999. This growth in number of

hosts is mind-boggling, particularly when considering that the individual hosts can serve many more individual users. 'World Wide Web' and 'Internet' have now become household terms; every day more and more people are accessing the Internet through academic, private, military, government, and commercial interests, primarily through networked computer systems.

Overview of Chapters

Chapter 2: What is the Internet?

This chapter outlines how secondary research can be carried out using the Internet.[4] An outline of available resources and procedures is presented, with emphasis upon both the time that can be saved, as compared with traditional (library-based) methods, and the additional information that can be accessed. However, the chapter also stresses the importance of assessing the relevance, quality, and reliability of these resources. The amount of information available is unfathomable and the researcher (and student) should be especially careful in ensuring that sources drawn upon are of high quality. Thus emphasis in this chapter is on providing guidelines for how to use the Internet effectively, and how to recognise bogus or limited sites.

The secondary information sources described include: subject-based discussion groups; library catalogues; newspapers; indexes to periodical literature; art archives; government official databases; and electronic texts. These sources provide a wealth of information relevant to many disciplines within the human sciences. The chapter explains how to use these resources, without assuming any prior familiarity. Thus detailed instructions are provided, often including a step-by-step account of the precise commands needed. Yet the chapter also provides valuable information for the user who may already have a basic familiarity with these resources, by providing recommendations for good practice, which can enhance efficiency and quality of materials gathered. Many readers will be familiar with using search engines to seek specific information, but will also be aware of the frustrations involved in having to trawl through volumes of useless information to find what is required. There are a number of alternative and extremely useful access points to information available, with which many researchers may be unfamiliar. These are described, with an emphasis on selecting those sites that are unlikely soon to go out of date. In summary, Chapter 2 gives a comprehensive introduction to the range and depth of information available on the

Internet (with a focus on that relevant to social and behavioural research), and how to access and test the quality of this information.

Chapter 3: Is the Internet a Viable Research Tool?

This chapter considers the extent to which the Internet opens up new possibilities for primary research in the social and behavioural sciences, in terms of both adapting existing methodologies and tools to a new medium, and creating new methodological possibilities. As well as outlining the range of methodologies and types of research that are practically possible, the chapter considers relevant theoretical, methodological, and ethical issues. Focus is on the extent to which Internet methodologies are able to produce valid and reliable data. Several concerns arise in relation to this issue. Sampling bias is an issue given lengthy consideration in this chapter (and re-addressed in later chapters). The claim assessed is that the Internet-user population constitutes an inherently biased sample of the population at large (in terms of sex, age, socioeconomic status, for example). Thus any studies that sample from this user population are severely limited in terms of generalisability and hence data validity. This is seen by some as a fundamental problem for Internet-mediated research. We do not agree, and this chapter explains why. The chapter also explores the types of sampling strategies that are available in IMR, and highlights how these interact with the types of samples that can be obtained. Recommendations for procedures that maximise data quality are given. The chapter also considers ethical issues in IMR, and provides suggestions for making sure that these are properly addressed.

The range of methodologies available in IMR is discussed in terms of the scope for adapting existing techniques and tools, as well as the novelties that an Internet medium can afford. Thus the advantages and disadvantages of Internet-based implementations are considered, compared to traditional methods. Some of the features of Internet-based primary research are access to larger and more diverse samples, reduced costs, and reduced timescale. In addition, the Internet allows entirely anonymous communication, but with higher levels of interactivity than has previously been possible. Further, IMR opens up new possibilities for unobtrusive observational research. These and other features of IMR are discussed. Caveats are also addressed. A major concern is the reduced level of researcher control (over participants, materials, and procedures) that IMR procedures often entail. Issues relating to current technological limitations, as well as demands for technological expertise of both researcher and participant, are also considered. The ways in which all these issues can impact upon IMR are discussed. Solutions are offered, though these await more detailed elaboration (in terms of the tools and procedures available) in subsequent chapters. Overall, the chapter provides a basic introduction to Internet-mediated primary research, outlining the scope, possibilities, and issues that arise.

Chapter 4: Equipment for Internet-Based Research

This chapter attempts to summarise the main technological issues and facilities relevant to IMR. Because the Internet is constructed around standard protocols, there are many competing software packages with overlapping ranges of functionality, implemented on a range of different hardware platforms, and this diversity poses problems for the design of reliable research paradigms. It is argued that, nevertheless, reasonable consistency across platforms is possible with care, but that there are some research questions that are better carried out in more controlled situations, even if they still make use of Internet technologies. The chapter proceeds to review the main classes of Internet technologies relevant to primary research, namely Telnet and FTP (File Transfer Protocol), Mail and USENET News, Internet chat systems, multimedia and the World Wide Web.

Owing to the complexity and power of Web technology, it is examined in special detail, with discussion of client-side and server-side technologies, and of the way they can be made to interact to create powerful systems for surveys and experimental studies. HTML (HyperText Markup Language), JavaScript, Java, and other proprietary technologies are discussed with emphasis on their usefulness for interface construction, ease of development, and security. The problem of establishing the identity of participants is addressed in the context of Web technology and contemporary modes of Internet access, and common technological approaches to the problem, such as the use of cookies, are critically examined. The chapter concludes with a discussion of the need for simple, robust design, if a system is to be widely accessible, and of the special importance of interface transparency in research contexts. Chapter 5 provides working examples of some of the Web technologies, in the hope that interested readers with little or no experience in Web development can be assisted to begin experimenting with systems of their own.

Chapter 5: How to Design and Implement an Internet Survey

This chapter gives details on how to get a Web-based survey up and running (email survey procedures are also discussed). Design issues are covered and, based on the empirical evidence available at the time of writing, along with our own insights, a set of design recommendations is

offered. Software procedures are outlined, and examples of programming code are given. By following the guidelines in this chapter the
reader should (presuming access to the necessary equipment) be able to
produce a well-designed survey that can be emailed to participants, or
posted on the World Wide Web, and that incorporates some of the
principles of good practice (such as debriefing, participant tracking,
informed consent) that have been emphasised throughout this book.

Chapter 6: What Can Go Wrong?

This chapter revisits many of the issues from earlier chapters, particularly issues of sampling from Chapter 3 and on instrumentation from
Chapter 4. Failures of Internet instrumentation and methodology are
considered, as are issues of etiquette and vandalism. The main issues at
stake are selecting the right level of technology for the research question
at hand. Instrumentation includes issues of both hardware and software,
as well as technical expertise of researcher and participants. The more
technically involved the experiment, the fewer researchers are actually
able to construct them in a properly controlled fashion, and the fewer
potential participants there are to involve in the research. The methodological issues focus mainly on pieces of information that are required
from Internet participants to potentially balance the quality of information they offer to the research. Issues here cover facts like whether
participants can touch type and whether they have Internet and/or email
access for free. However, there are additional facts about timing the call
for participants and deciding how to distribute that call. The latter
interacts with issues of etiquette, what appropriate ways of attracting
participants might be. We point out some common pitfalls and suggest
solutions. Finally we consider the issue of hackers, whether random
hackers or those moving under the mask of bona fide participants. We
make some suggestions about file location, password protection, and
user accounts generally. We stress throughout maximal researcher control over materials and data. This might seem to suggest that researchers
should become competent programmers, able to design their own programs to manage Internet research. However, we fall shy of suggesting
that, preferring the alternative strategy discussed in the instrumentation
section: that of using experiment servers provided on the Web for non-
programmers to construct and conduct studies over the Internet.

Chapter 7: Case Studies

This chapter presents three case studies, from the authors' own research,
that demonstrate and elucidate many of the issues discussed throughout
the preceding chapters. The first case study is a good example of a very

simple (in terms of requiring minimal equipment and technical expertise) implementation, which made use of USENET newsgroups to contact and recruit participants, and email to administer materials and collect responses. The procedure is described, along with a discussion of problems that arose, and suggestions for improvements.[5] Case study 2 describes a more complex implementation, which made use of the World Wide Web to deliver materials and collect data.[6] Problems that arose with the initial design of the study are highlighted, and the technical solutions developed to resolve these problems described. This study provides a good illustration of the use of several of the tools and procedures discussed in Chapter 3. The third case study is another example of IMR that is relatively straightforward to implement, requiring no specialist knowledge of computing. In this case the procedure involved participants conversing with each other via email (in pairs). The email interactions themselves did not constitute the primary data for the study, rather the researcher was interested in participants' subsequent reports of their experiences during these email dialogues. An evaluation of the initial implementation is presented, along with a description of later developments and modifications. Many of the issues raised throughout the book are recapitulated here.

These case studies are useful in further illustrating the points raised throughout the book, and provide useful and informative demonstrations of Internet-mediated research in action. Lessons to be learned are highlighted.

In conclusion, this book covers a range of theoretical, methodological and practical issues involved in using the Internet to conduct primary research in the social and behavioural sciences. Using this book as a guide, the practising researcher should be well equipped to conduct a well-designed research study on the Internet. The information needed to be able to select appropriate sampling procedures, adhere to ethical guidelines, and maximise data validity is provided. Most importantly, the book makes Internet research available to researchers without the need for acquisition of advanced computing skills. Throughout the book we emphasise the great potential for the Internet to enhance and facilitate research across a wide range of research domains. We urge readers to make use of this potential in their own research.

Notes

1 Which we consider to include (amongst others) psychology, linguistics, sociology, economics, political science, cognitive science, and anthropology.
2 These procedures are very easy to get to grips with, for readers who are not already familiar. Any introductory guide to the Internet should provide instructions (for example, Kennedy, 2001; Kent, 2001; Lehnert, 1998).

3   These packages tend to focus on implementing studies via the World Wide Web (WWW). This is because other Internet tools, such as email, Telnet, FTP, USENET (described in later chapters) are somewhat easier to use for the non-expert, whereas constructing a WWW study requires considerably more programming expertise, and knowledge of computer systems.

4   The reader is referred also to O'Dochartaigh (2001), which is complementary to the current book, though at a somewhat lower (undergraduate) level.

5   This study was actually conducted before the wave of interest in Internet-mediated research methodologies, and thus did not benefit from the types of guidelines that have since been presented.

6   This approach is discussed at length in Chapters 4 and 5.

2
What is the Internet?

Research on the Internet begins like any other research. Possible research areas are explored until a final topic is settled on; the reliability of sources is judged. Solid information is gathered, a working bibliography is framed, and databases at research centres are accessed. Using traditional research methods, it is possible to spend countless hours in the library, interviewing sources, and combing through card catalogues, journals, and indexes, while on the Internet a university or organization probably already has a web page on the topic selected, making information retrieval easier from one central location, a home computer.

Thousands of library catalogues, including all major university research libraries, are easily accessible online. Online catalogues allow a search by author, title, or subject, facilitating the compilation of a working bibliography in much less time than is required for traditional methods. The Internet has a searchable online database of thousands of journals and tables of contents. With all research, it is important to learn how to find information without wasting time. The best way to achieve this goal is to learn how to use the Internet search and discovery tools and to evaluate the findings in terms of relevance, quality, and reliability.

Our goal is not to list URLs (Uniform Resource Locators) that will change before this book is in print for a year, but to provide strategies for finding sites that are not likely to be outdated soon because of their quality, relevance, and reliability. This chapter describes various sources for secondary information available over the Internet.

The Internet makes longitudinal study more practically feasible and enables a more comprehensive search than was possible before its widespread use. Without much direct contact with primary sources, a researcher can still connect with many individuals from different locations interested in the same topic to access information held in common.

It is impossible to work comfortably on the Internet without established guidelines for judging the reliability of web pages. Being proficient at judging the reliability of a site is important because the frequent change and reconstruction of sites renders it a daily and recurrent task. The first step in establishing reliability of a web page is to search the Web for the author's name. If a biographical link is available, follow it. An author's homepage will sometimes contain helpful information such as education, affiliations, and body of work. The goal is to establish the author's qualifications; in other words, is the author an authority in the field? The next stage in judging reliability is to see if the site represents other sources fairly. Check the resources to see if there is adequate information and if that information gives a fair hearing of the topic. Next check the accuracy of data at a particular source by following links to cited sources. And as simply as if doing library research, check the currency of the site. What is the date on the material? When was the material last updated? When was the web page last updated? The ability to recognize bogus or limited sites quickly enables the researcher to spend time efficiently. It is important always to keep in mind that data are not knowledge. The inexhaustible distribution of data on the Internet has proceeded at a greater rate than its rational organization or coherence. Researchers have to overcome these problems when deciding the usability of a site.

The Web allows different search objectives. Any topic or subject can be researched. Corporate and commercial information has inundated the Internet. Both public domain and shareware programs can be downloaded. Directories of individuals can be utilised to contact people, while special-interest groups can be contacted through discussion groups and lists. This chapter looks at different resources for social science[1] search areas.

The range of secondary sources available for researchers includes, but is not limited to:

- subject-based discussion groups;
- library catalogues;
- newspapers;
- indexes to periodical literature;
- art archives;
- government official databases; and
- electronic texts including literature

Subject-Based Discussion Groups

Electronic discussion groups (also known as listservs) are made up of people interested in a common subject or area of discussion who form a distribution list of their email addresses. Members of the group can send a message and have it automatically distributed to everyone on the list. Administrative functions such as subscribing and unsubscribing (that is, joining or leaving) are generally automated. Email is the lowest common denominator of network access. Even if a user does not have Web access, the user can still have email access. Consequently, email-based electronic discussion groups have been among the most popular and successful of all academically oriented Internet tools. Thousands of different email discussion groups exist on almost every topic imaginable. Messages are typically announcements, questions, statements, or replies to other members. To receive a listserv's posting, a subscription request must be sent to the listserv from an email account.

Listservs include open lists where anyone may subscribe and post messages, moderated lists where a human moderator reviews messages before they are sent to the group, and closed lists where permission must be requested to join. Consult a mailing list directory such as the one at *www.liszt.com* for an extensive list and description of thousands of different listservs by topic. Another option is to browse a catalogue of listservs by accessing *www.lsoft.com*.

To contact a list of lists by email, send an email to *listserv@listserv.net*. Leave the subject line blank. In the body of your email write 'list global'. The document you receive from the listserv will be very long. For a shorter, more manageable list narrow your search by changing 'list global' in the body to 'list global/topic' where 'topic' is replaced with the subject you are interested in reading.

After subscribing, save the confirmation letter because it contains information about sending messages, contacting the listowner, suspending messages for a day or two, and unsubscribing from the listserv. Some confirmation letters will also give information on where to find the FAQs (Frequently Asked Questions) for the list. Answers to questions about the netiquette (etiquette of the online group) observed by each particular group are usually found in the FAQ.

After joining a list, monitor the messages for a week or so to get a feel for the community. What topics are considered appropriate to each group will become clear, and the group dynamic will be apparent to the newcomer in a short time. Ask for private responses when appropriate since not all messages need to go to all group members. Do not clutter the listserv with off-subject messages, and reduce the number of duplicate responses by replying privately. Another important piece of advice is to delete extraneous text when responding to previous posting.

Netiquette or etiquette on the Net prescribes some simple rules. Since tone and attitude are not easily discerned in a written message, it is important that the writer give clues to the reader about the intent of a post. Some important standards apply: for instance, using all caps means that the writer is being emphatic, even yelling. It is considered poor form. End all email with your name and email address to make it easier for others to respond. Always give a subject heading to posts, unless sending messages to list software for administrative purposes. Crosspost – that is, send a message from one list to another – only if the subject of the post will be of interest to the group. Examples of acceptable messages

to crosspost are announcements of conferences, internships, or job vacan-
cies. Warnings about viruses usually turn out to be false and should not
be crossposted.

Practise conciseness when using email. Messages need not be short,
but they should be to the point. People have little time and lots of email
to read. Wordiness only muddies the message. Be tolerant of errors in the
messages posted. Absolutely nobody wants grammar or spelling errors
pointed out to them. Unless an error makes the message unintelligible,
figure out what the writer meant and move on. If the post is unintelligible, reply privately to the writer, or wait for the poster to resubmit
the message. Only quote the portion of a previous post that is necessary
for understanding the message that you write. Long or full quotes waste
space and time.

Since the primary goal of the Internet is communication, it is important not to inadvertently offend others who are members of the listserv.
Also, be aware that what seems like a great and clever retort can end up
being an embarrassing mistake when posted to thousands of readers on
a listserv and then indexed for millions to read in the archives. So give
yourself time to think through what you are writing. Finally, do not
engage in flaming or flame wars. A flame is a message that is an angry
reply to a posted email message. If you feel the need to reply to a flame,
do so privately, and keep it off-list.

Library Catalogues

Most research begins in a library. But it is no longer necessary to go to the
physical structure to get information needed on a particular topic. Online
searches of library holdings are possible in a fraction of the time it takes
to search in the traditional way. Library catalogues provide an index to
materials owned by a particular institution. Searches are usually done by
author, title, or subject. The full text of the material will not usually be
accessible, although it is sometimes possible to find full texts of some
sources.

When querying a library catalogue, the results received are often
pieces of information about a physical resource of the library, rather than
the resource itself, though libraries are now adding some full-text
indexing features to their catalogues. While library catalogues may not
provide indexes to journal articles themselves, the journal titles will be
provided. Few library catalogues provide indexes to journal articles, and
when these catalogues are available it is usually only for the students,
faculty, and staff of the university where the catalogue is located, not to
every Internet user. So, specific journal articles will probably be easier to
find using electronic or paper indexes, most of which are not publicly

available on the Internet but are still common in libraries. A couple of the electronic indexes are discussed later.

Searching a library catalogue is done for one of three reasons: to locate a book, journal or other material to check out of the library; to find bibliographic information; and to see what books or journals are available on a particular topic or by a particular author. Searching a library catalogue by Internet is not done to retrieve the material electronically, but to find out the availability of sources on a particular topic.

One problem with accessing library catalogues is that many types of software are used from site to site, each with its own command language. Many institutions modify their software to reflect their own needs, so that the same program may look different from site to site. Fortunately, library catalogues are designed to make searches easy to accommodate people with different levels of computer expertise.

Finding Library Catalogues with HYTELNET

Library catalogues can be difficult to use on computer. Usually the first step is to access the homepage of a university and then look for a link to its library catalogue. Each library catalogue looks a little different and many have a unique set of commands. If the university catalogue you have access to does not have the information necessary, HYTELNET, a directory of libraries developed by Peter Scott at the University of Saskatchewan Libraries, is a good place to start.

HYTELNET is a tool that helps bring Internet-accessible library catalogues into a single directory and provides some direction for using the catalogues. It provides a directory of library catalogues and uses Telnet to access them. The HYTELNET information page (*www.lights.com/hytelnet*) gives information about updates, client software, and changes. The main menu leads to several options for information including: Help files for library catalogues, Internet glossary, Telnet tips, and resources such as library catalogues and community information systems and bulletin boards, and specific texts and graphics databases.

Using HYTELNET

With a web browser, go to *moondog.usask.ca/*. Once at this site follow the link 'Library Catalogues'. From here follow the link 'The Americas'. Now look at libraries in the United States by following the link 'Type of Library'. Next follow the link 'Academics, Research, and General Libraries'. Then, scroll down until you find the library you would like to search. This link will give the following information: the Telnet address to access the catalogue; an indication if a user name is required or the appropriate login name to use; an indication of the software used and a link to the software information with a summary of search commands; and the command used to exit from the library catalogue when finished. Since it is necessary to know information about the search commands for the software the library has chosen, first follow the link to the catalogue software. Using a web browser, go back to the previous page: the library selected. To connect to the library catalogue, follow the link. If it is a Telnet connection, type in the terminal type being used. Type 'Y' to confirm the choice. Then type 'A' to search by author. An introductory screen will appear. Type in the author using the example of how to enter author names. Press 'Enter'. The books and their call numbers are listed. Type the number of the item you are interested in for more information about that item.

Newspapers

LEXIS-NEXIS

LEXIS-NEXIS (*www.lexis-nexis.com*) contains the full text of thousands of newspapers, reports, and journals. If you were in the library you would connect to NEXIS, while LEXIS is a database of legal information, used by law offices and law students for research. Comprehensive information on which publications are indexed and provided by LEXIS-NEXIS is available from their homepage. LEXIS-NEXIS works by allowing searches of the information, using a search language that provides full Boolean search features for refining queries (Boolean operators are the words: 'and', 'or', 'not'. When these words are placed between key-words, they expand or limit the scope of the search.) The News library contains the full text of more than 2,300 newspapers, news wires, newsletters, and broadcast transcripts. Publications range from *The New York Times* to *Western Morning News* to *The Moscow Times*. After searching on LEXIS-NEXIS, results can be displayed, saved, or printed as full text of the articles to the citations of the articles. This database is expensive; however, most libraries have access to it. Since it is a comprehensive source for current news or business information, it is a valuable resource.

Check out these newspapers online:

Detroit Free Press	*www.freep.com*
The Guardian – UK	*www.guardian.co.uk*
The Irish Times	*www.ireland.com*
The New York Times	*www.nytimes.com/*
San Francisco Chronicle	*www.sfgate.com*
The Washington Post	*www.washingtonpost.com*

Dow Jones News/Retrieval

Dow Jones News/Retrieval (*www.lib.virginia.edu/indexes/dowjones.html*) is another commercial information service like LEXIS-NEXIS also available on the Internet, but it is also expensive. Accessing it through a library or college is an option in many places. Its focus is business and financial news.

American City Business Journals

American City Business Journals (*www.bizjournals.com*) searches the archives of specialised business newspapers from 35 United States cities.

Indexes to Periodical Literature

Document delivery refers to the electronic transmission of journal articles. Document delivery developed not only for its convenience to the user, but also because libraries cannot afford to subscribe to every journal that students, faculty and staff might need. Most libraries subscribe to many core journals and to a commercial document delivery service that can transmit articles from the journals not in their collection.

Many document delivery services still do not send the requested documents by computer. So even if a document is requested via computer, the article is usually faxed. There are many document delivery services available to libraries, but one of the most useful is Ingenta. Ingenta follows from UnCover which began as a service of CARL, a consortium of Colorado libraries. In 2001, Ingenta purchased UnCover and merged their databases and services. It is a database of current article information taken from over 18,000 multi-disciplinary journals. The database contains brief bibliographic information for over 11 million articles published from autumn 1988 to the present. REVEAL, a service also on the Ingenta page, is an automated alerting service that delivers the tables of contents of selected journals directly to your email box. The REVEAL service also allows users to create and enter search strategies for topics.

UnCover is available over the Internet and can be useful even without paying for full text articles. UnCover can browse the tables of contents of many journals in all areas of study, search for the article titles, journal titles, and names of the authors, and request that an article be faxed (with a credit card and payment or an affiliation with a university that subsidises the cost of the service). The cost per journal article is for the copyright fee and the faxing and varies depending on the length of the article and publisher.

Although Ingenta is useful, less expensive options are often preferred. Libraries can usually get documents delivered through various inter-library loan sources free of charge to the patron, although the process can take three to ten days. Most articles that are available through Ingenta for faxing are sent within 48 hours. Articles with a clock icon are available within one hour while articles designated with a computer icon are available for desktop delivery within one to 24 hours. Articles available for faxing or desktop delivery will be designated 'Mark for Order'. An article already available in the library may be designated 'Held by Library', and may not be faxed under a subsidy. Articles 'Not Held' may be ordered through traditional Interlibrary Loan by clicking on 'Email citation' when the article information is displayed.

Sometimes faxing of an article is not allowed because of the copyright. In such a case, an inter-library loan can be made. The library's inter-library loan fax number is generally the default, so articles are picked up in the inter-library loan office, but the default can be changed to a personal or department fax machine in the profile.

Ingenta can be accessed either from the CARL homepage or from the library homepage of a particular university. If the library homepage has an Ingenta page, click on 'Connect to Ingenta'. First time and off-campus users must obtain a username and password, but only people associated with the university can get this information; further, often only university faculty, staff, and graduate students are allowed to charge their document delivery requests to the library's deposit account.

The Ingenta homepage (*www.ingenta.com*) provides access to the UnCover plus document delivery service and information and access to other databases. A password is needed to access most of the databases provided through Ingenta. Researchers with library privileges at a university should ask the librarian for the password.

To access the UnCover plus service, follow these steps. From the Ingenta gateway homepage, choose Ingenta UnCover. From the next page, choose 'The UnCover Homepage'. Information about the UnCover service can be obtained from the UnCover homepage. To connect to UnCover, follow the link 'Click here' to access the UnCover database. Telnet is automatically invoked and connects to the UnCover system. Choose a terminal type to continue. Next, choose from the databases listed. Unfortunately, almost all of them require a password, so the researcher can access only those databases to which the library sub-scribes. Type '1' and press 'Enter' to access UnCover. If you do not have a password, press 'Enter' and press 'Enter' again to continue. You are prompted to enter a profile number that will speed up future use of this service. Press 'Enter' to continue. At this point you set up a profile. Again, press 'Enter'. The UnCover main menu should appear. This is where to begin the search. To search by word in the journal title, article title, or subject area, use the 'W' command. The 'N' command allows a search for an author's name. The 'B' command is to search for a particular journal title, and to browse the titles and authors of the journal chosen.

As mentioned, Ingenta includes back issues only to around 1988 and so is most useful for more recent articles. The bottom of the screen gives the available options. The meaning of different options is not always clear, and which choice is the right one is not always apparent. To browse the journals choose 'E'. A sample table of contents will be next. Menu items at the bottom of the screen allow the marking of any of the articles for delivery. For more details about the article itself, simply type the number of the article. Once documents are marked for ordering, type the letter 'O', and wait for the prompt to enter credit card and address information. There is some risk in transmitting credit card numbers over the Internet so it is important to think about online safety. Always use a secure browser that complies with industry security standards, such as Secure Sockets Layer (SSL) or Secure Electronic Transaction (SET). These standards encrypt information, ensuring the security of each transaction. Most computers come with a browser already installed. Another option is to download a browser. Be sure, also, to keep a record by printing a copy of the transaction with a confirmation number. Fortunately, CARL can be contacted by telephone to set up a profile so that personal account numbers do not have to be divulged via the Internet.

Once you have a profile number you may Telnet directly to UnCover. The Telnet address is *database.carl.org*. After establishing the Telnet connection, you will be prompted for the terminal type, then for the password. Press return until you are prompted for your profile number. From here follow the prompts to access information.

It is not necessary to use the document delivery feature of Ingenta to benefit from the service. Searching for journal articles with Ingenta can be useful and will not cost anything. Ingenta can be useful to check bibliographic information so that articles are cited correctly. The Ingenta helpdesk can be contacted in the UK: help@ingenta.com and in the US: ushelp@ingenta.com

REVEAL

REVEAL is an automated alerting service that delivers tables of contents from selected journals to an email account. In the REVEAL Search profile, the researcher selects a list of titles, keywords, author's name, or a combination. This list is run against the Ingenta database. If Ingenta finds an article or journal that matches the list of terms or titles, an email message with information about matching articles is sent.

REVEAL is also available through the Ingenta page. Again, a username and password are required and should be obtained from the library staff. At some universities only faculty and staff can use the service and users must register by first setting up a profile in Ingenta. Articles can be ordered through REVEAL by replying to REVEAL alert email messages. Place the word 'ORDER' next to the order number of the desired articles. Researchers associated with a university may have articles subsidised by the library. This subsidy is often available only to faculty and staff.[2]

Art Archives

Websites from international museums to local galleries designed to educate and entertain both the serious art student and the casual art lover can be found on the Internet. Many art museums offer everything from basic background information on a particular artist to sophisticated virtual-technology tours of a museum's entire collection. There are even online art museums that exist only on the World Wide Web. Art museums around the world are open 24 hours a day, seven days a week, to anyone with Internet access. Using the Web to learn about art allows the researcher to more easily follow an artist, a line of interest, school, or movement than if using the traditional method of art books and classes.

Some museums present their stellar art objects, while others display lesser known works and feature historical information. For information about an artist, it is easy to perform a keyword search on a web browser and download all the material.

Several national museums offer multimedia tours of their collections. The National Gallery of Art (USA) site (*www.nga.gov*) offers a comprehensive virtual tour of over 100,000 objects, including major accomplishments in painting, sculpture, and graphic arts from the Middle Ages to the present. The collection can be searched by specific artist or title or by medium and school. Tours are offered in several languages, including French, Spanish, German, Italian and English.

Visit these online art museums:

Galleria degli Uffizi	Florence	*www.uffizi.firenze.it/*
The Hermitage	Russia	*www.hermitagemuseum.org*
The Louvre	Paris	*www.louvre.fr/*
Metropolitan Museum of Art	New York	*www.metmuseum.org/home.asp*
The Minneapolis Institute of Arts	Minneapolis	*www.artsmia.org*
Museum of Contemporary Art	San Diego	*www.mcasd.org*
The Museum of Fine Arts Boston	Boston	*www.mfa.org*
National Gallery of Art	Washington	*www.nga.gov*
The Smithsonian	Washington	*www.si.edu*

To learn about Van Gogh at this site, begin by clicking on 'Virtual Exhibition Tours' and then choose between the plugin and non-plugin tour. Technical requirements for both tours are described. The plugin tour allows a visual walk through of the rooms of the gallery, clicking on paintings for larger image views, details and more information. Directions tell how to use the keyboard to zoom in and out and find important viewpoints. Details on the art work and Van Gogh's life can be heard by clicking on the RealAudio file. The non-plugin tour, while fixed, allows the user to select and enlarge paintings and also obtain information.

The National Gallery of Art homepage also gives the options of Collection Tours, In-Depth Study Tours, and Architecture Tours. Artists included in the in-depth tours are Edouard Manet, Thomas Moran, Jackson Pollock, Mark Rothko and Alfred Stieglitz. The Stieglitz tour includes an overview, biography, featured photographs, and techniques.

The Louvre online (*www.louvre.fr/*) features the history and collection of more than 6,000 European paintings dating from the late thirteenth to the mid-nineteenth century. A user can view both the exterior and the interior of the building complex by choosing the virtual tour mode. The plugin QuickTime will have to be downloaded to view close-up. Use the keyboard to zoom in, or click and drag the mouse to get a 360-degree view of the room and all of its masterpieces.

Researchers interested in how art masterpieces are cleaned and restored should go to the Minneapolis Institute of Arts site (*www.artsmia. org*) and use its Restoration Online feature. The daily progress of a recent restoration is featured as well as background materials on the work. This site requires QuickTime and Flash downloads.

A virtual museum, *ArtMuseum.net*, is an extension, not a replacement, of the physical art museum. ArtMuseum.net encourages visitors to become members, requiring only the completion of a questionnaire to gain access to additional content, including audio, advance information on upcoming exhibits, and a discount at the ArtMuseum.net store.

Various contemporary artists have curated a virtual collection of art shows by members who wish to share their works via the Internet. Art on the Net (*www.art.net*) is a non-commercial site. The homepage lists links and what they offer. Various artists have studios listed under the categories: Digital Artists, Hacker Artists, Musicians and Bands, Painters, Performance Artists, Photographers, Poets, Sculptors, Video Artists and Animators, and Visual Artists.

An excellent site for information about museums on the Web is the World Wide Web Virtual Library Museums page supported by the International Council of Museums (*www.icom.org/vlmp/*). The list is split into sub-lists by country or region. Once you choose a country, museums are listed alphabetically with links directly to each museum. This site lists all types of museums from planetariums to virtual library zoos.

Government Official Databases

UK online

Run by the Office of the e-Envoy, part of the Cabinet Office, UK online (*www.ukonline.gov.uk*) provides access to over 1,000 government websites on the Internet. Content may be viewed in either English or Welsh and covers England, Northern Ireland, Scotland and Wales. Do it Online gives you direct access to services such as completing a tax return or a passport application online, finding a tradesman to work in your home, or finding suitable childcare in your local area. In CitizenSpace information on voting and elections, representatives and how to complain about public services can be found. Logging in here will enable you to take part in discussion groups. Yourlife supplies guidance, advice and support through life events such as having a baby, searching for a job, dealing with death and grief. Perhaps the most helpful section is Quick find where you can search a range of websites by theme.

THOMAS

THOMAS (*thomas.loc.gov*) is one of the most valuable sources on US legislation. THOMAS covers legislation, congressional record, and committee information. THOMAS provides information about the activities of the United States Congress, including the full text of all bills and legislation. This information can be searched by type of bill and by keyword in the text of the bill. A feature called 'Congress in the News' directs the user to bills in the media that are most frequently referred to and those most often requested from legislative librarians.

THOMAS contains legislation as far back as 1992. The following databases are offered by THOMAS: House Floor This Week, House Floor Now, Quick Search of Text of Bills. Under Legislation a researcher will find: Bill Summary and Status, Bill Text from 101st to 106th Congresses (1989-2000), Major Legislation since 1995, Public Laws by Law Number, and Votes (House Roll Call Votes and Senate Roll Call Votes).

In Congressional Record, you will find Most Recent Issue, Congressional Record Text, Congressional Record Index, Resumés of

---

Visit these government resources:

The Library of Congress	*lcweb.loc.gov/*
The U.S. Department of Education	*www.ed.gov/*
The White House	*www.whitehouse.gov*

Congressional Activity, and Days in Session Calendars. Under Committee Information you will find Committee Reports, Committee Home Pages, House Committees, and Senate Committees. It contains the text of new bills within 48 hours.

In addition to THOMAS databases, the THOMAS homepage provides links to The Legislative Process, Historical Documents, US Congressional Documents and Debates: 1774–1873, House and Senate Directories, and Library of Congress Web Links.

LOCIS

LOCIS (*www.galaxy.com/hytelnet/US373.html*), the Library of Congress Information System, is a database of about 12 million records representing books, serials, computer files, manuscripts, cartographic materials, music, sound recordings, and visual materials in the Library's collection. It provides information about books and non-print materials catalogued by the Library of Congress, federal legislation, copyrighted materials registered with the Library of Congress, Braille and audio materials, bibliographies for people doing basic research, and foreign law material. The Library of Congress does not provide the full text of the materials. Since most of the materials are copyrighted, they must be purchased or found in a library if you want to use them. The system is useful for retrieving information about published work that you will get from the library.

FedWorld

FedWorld (*www.fedworld.gov*) is a website maintained by the National Technical Information Service of the United States government. It offers multiple distribution channels to provide information links to reports from all agencies of the US government. FedWorld is useful for a variety of research needs including policy statements or analysis, scientific data, and geological information. The FedWorld homepage links to federal government information servers.This site offers a comprehensive central access point from which to search for, locate, order, and acquire government and business information. It has full text of many databases, including: Foreign News Alert Service, Supreme Court Decisions, 1937–1975, Wage Determination Act Database, and the Clean Air Act Database. Meta-Databases (systems that point to the actual data or how to get it) include US Federal Government Job Announcements, Descriptions of IRS Tax Forms, and Descriptions of 12,000 Federal Aviation Administration Files, among many others.

Electronic Texts Including Literature

Although every researcher has respect for books – the weight of the volume, the feel of the page, the smell of the leather binding on an older edition – we have begun the shift from print to digital form. Nothing can replace the satisfaction of a fine edition, but there is also a need for quick and easy access to a growing mass of digital material.

Project Gutenberg

Many electronic text archives, such as those maintained by Project Gutenberg (*promo.net/pg/*), are composed of works in the public domain. Project Gutenberg began in 1971 when Michael Hart was given free computer time, which he decided to use by creating a file of online electronic texts. The philosophy of the project directors is to make information, books, and other materials available to the general public in forms that can be easily read, used, quoted, and searched.

Project Gutenberg is divided into three sections: Light Literature, Heavy Literature, and References. It is easy to look up quotations heard in movies, music or other books because of the easy to find e-text format. From the homepage, it is easy to browse the Index/Catalogue by title and author or to use the search engine to find and download books. Also the whole list of Project Gutenberg books is available as a plain text file or a zip file. Step-by-step directions are given on how to get books via FTP and the Web and how to subscribe to the listservs. A help page is also provided at this site.

The On-Line Books Page (*digital.library.upenn.edu/books/*) is another helpful site. Its homepage offers a search engine of over 10,000 listings. Searches can be conducted by author or title. Search results provide links to the texts.

In conclusion, it is easy to become familiar with a full range of secondary sources available on the Internet. The learning curve for becoming proficient in any one area is certainly worth the time saved when looking at long-term study in a particular field. As in any research, countless hours can be spent, but by fine-tuning the focus of your investigation, becoming efficient in online computer skills, and making an effort not to get lost in the innumerable links to fascinating, but useless, information, research can be accurate, appropriate, and efficient. A caution, parallel to the one stated at the outset of this chapter about verifying the reliability of an Internet resource, is to avoid the assumption that information not easily found on the Internet does not exist. Traditional libraries will not disappear.

Notes

1 We use the term 'social science' for brevity, though, as explained in the Introduction, the issues raised in this book are relevant to a range of disciplines in what may broadly be termed the social, behavioural and human sciences.

2 In addition to articles available this way, or through direct library subscriptions to electronic copies of journals, in some disciplines (for example, linguistics and computer science) it is common practice for researchers to make pre-print versions of their papers electronically available in their own web pages or those of their research group. In this way, articles are freely available to anyone who has a computer that can download them. Similarly, it is not uncommon within a discipline for there to be electronic archives of papers, also freely available to anyone. For example, the URL *xxx.lanl.gov/* provides access to a range of archives in physics, mathematics, and areas broadly identified as computing, but inclusive of computational linguistics. Similarly, papers in cognitive science are available from *cogprints.soton.ac.uk/*. Other subject areas are similarly codified, and freely available.

3
Is the Internet a Viable Research Tool?

The previous chapter's focus was on the ways in which the Internet can be used as a secondary research tool in the social sciences. A range of resources were outlined along with instructions on how to use them. This chapter is concerned with the scope of the Internet for use in conducting primary social scientific research. The chapter serves as a preliminary introduction, outlining a range of issues that are taken up in more detail in later chapters. We consider the types of methodologies that might be adapted to an Internet-mediated approach, types of data that can be collected, and research areas that may benefit. We also outline the advantages and limitations of IMR approaches, as compared with more traditional methods.

However, before addressing these questions we feel it is necessary to spend some time discussing the issue of Internet samples. A common initial reaction to the suggestion that the Internet may provide a valuable new resource for conducting primary research in the social sciences is that the Internet provides us with an inherently biased and select sample. The claim is that the Internet-user population consists primarily of well-educated, high-earning, technologically proficient males who work in computer, academic, or other professional fields. We carefully consider this issue as it is of fundamental importance to the whole notion of Internet-based research. We argue that overall the evidence suggests that the Internet-user population represents a vast and diverse section of the general population that is rapidly moving beyond the select group of technologically proficient professionals who were once largely predominant. Further, the type of sampling procedures used will influence the nature of the samples obtained. We consider the alternatives available and provide recommendations for obtaining samples appropriate to the particular research goals.

Sampling from the Internet-User Population

An often stated claim (from our experience of informal discussions about Internet-mediated data collection with practicing researchers) is that the Internet-user population constitutes a dramatically skewed sample of the 'population at large' and for this reason Internet-mediated research is immediately subject to serious problems concerning sample representativeness and validity of data. This view has also been widely expressed within the literature in this area (for example, Bordia, 1996; Coomber, 1997a; Schmidt, 1997; Stanton, 1998; Szabo and Frenkl, 1996). Szabo and Frenkl, for example, report statistics from a WWW-user survey (Parallax, 1996) and conclude that '[t]hese figures are fairly self-explanatory. The Internet researcher, for now, has to base his or her results on an upper middle-class and well-educated population mainly from the United States' (1996, p. 62). Bordia warns that '[i]n spite of the growing number of people who use computer communication, computers are still available to only a certain segment of the population' (1996, p. 150).

More recently this view has been challenged. This must be at least in part due to actual changes that are taking place. The continued explosive growth of the Internet is increasingly apparent. The volume and diversity of information available on the Internet have been demonstrated in Chapter 2. However, the resources described there constitute a mere fraction of what is in fact available. It is now possible to use the Internet to (amongst other things) buy, sell, view houses, check the weather forecast, view television schedules, pay bills, manage bank accounts, obtain insurance quotes, book hotel rooms, buy travel tickets, and seek a partner. One could argue that not having Internet access in the current climate is a disadvantage, or at least may become so in the near future if the current growth rate continues. Thus it is indisputable that the use of the Internet in business, education, communication, recreation, and for commercial purposes is becoming more and more widespread. Correspondingly, both the number and diversity of Internet users are increasing, facilitated by the availability of cheap Internet-capable computers.

While the above considerations are persuasive in damping concerns about sampling bias and the Internet-user population, a number of studies are now emerging that explicitly address the issue of Internet sample representativeness. For example, Smith and Leigh (1997) report a study that compares an Internet and non-Internet sample on several demographic variables. They found that the samples did not differ in terms of sexual orientation, marital status, ethnicity, education, and religiosity, but that they did differ in terms of age and sex. While sex and age are important variables, if anything these results appear to support the advantage of Internet over traditional samples since the Internet sample contained a wider age range, and whereas the Internet sample did show a bias towards male respondents (74 per cent male), the campus sample showed an even stronger bias in the opposite direction (80 per cent females). This result suggests a greater level of comparability between Internet and non-Internet samples than has previously been suggested (that is, in terms of five out of seven demographic variables), and also indicates that Internet samples may be more representative than traditional samples. However, conclusions from this set of results are limited since the samples obtained were selected in such a way that they would be expected to be similar: the Internet sample were volunteers who answered a posting to the *sci.psychology.research* newsgroup and the non-Internet sample consisted of undergraduate psychology students selected from a voluntary subject pool. The question remains as to whether a different Internet sampling procedure (for example, posting to the newsgroup *alt.sport.darts*) would have yielded similar results.

Further support for the enhanced diversity of Internet samples is provided by Krantz et al. (1997). They collected data on the determinants of female attractiveness from both a traditional undergraduate psychology student sample and a sample of volunteers accessed by posting participation requests to a psychology departmental homepage and the American Psychological Association online research page. The Web sample was found to have a wider age range, and to be more diverse in terms of race and country of origin (though participants in both samples were predominantly white North Americans). In contrast to Smith and Leigh's results, the samples were found to be comparable in terms of sex, males and females being roughly equally represented in both samples. Stanton (1998) supported the comparability of Internet and non-Internet samples on the sex variable, finding no significant difference between a sample recruited by email and a sample recruited from firms via telephone. Stanton's samples showed no significant differences in age. The over-representation of North Americans in Internet samples was supported by Browndyke et al.(1998), who obtained a sample of 260 volunteer participants who responded to postings to a range of USENET newsgroups requesting participation in a survey on head injury. Approximately 75 per cent of this sample were from North America, the next largest group coming from Europe. Kaye and Johnson (1999) conducted a political survey, and recruited a sample of 306 participants by posting participation requests to a number of politically based web sites, USENET newsgroups, listservs, and chat forums. They report their sample consisting primarily of white males with high education levels and high socioeconomic status.

The above results are inconclusive. There seems to be a tendency for Internet samples to have a wider age range and to be more ethnically diverse, and perhaps to contain more males than females. However, it seems apparent that the type of sample obtained will rely heavily on the sampling methodology employed, for both traditional and Internet samples. Levels of comparability between Internet and non-Internet samples will thus depend on the particular sampling procedures employed for both. Indeed it should not be presumed that similarity to traditional samples is a good measure of the validity of Internet samples – traditional samples are themselves often biased (for example, towards undergraduate students). If anything it seems that IMR, with careful consideration of appropriate sampling procedures, has the potential to offer access to a wider range of participants than has been traditionally readily available.

Further support for the validity of Internet sampling procedures comes from studies that have compared data from Internet and non-Internet samples. Buchanan and Smith (1999a) administered a personality test (Gangestead and Snyder's [1985] revised self-monitoring questionnaire) to an Internet and non-Internet sample and found that both sets of data displayed similar psychometric properties. However, this study recruited a non-Internet sample of undergraduate students and an Internet sample that consisted of participants most likely to have a particular interest in psychological research (volunteers to postings to *alt.usenet.surveys, sci.research, sci.psychology, alt.psychology.personality,* and *alt.psychology.help*), leaving open the question of the effects of using samples that extend beyond undergraduate students and those Internet users with a particular interest in psychological research. Interestingly, though, Buchanan and Smith report approximately equal numbers of males and females in their Internet sample (of 973 participants), which contrasted with their non-Internet sample (224 participants), which comprised about 80 per cent females. They also report a wider age range in the Internet sample, and responses from across the globe (according to respondents' Internet addresses). This again indicates the possible advantage of Internet samples.[1] Senior et al. (1999) also report wider age range and responses from around the globe in their Internet sample, as compared with a non-Internet sample that was predominantly British.

Szabo et al. (1996) targeted a rather different Internet sample (from undergraduates and those interested in psychology), posting requests for participation in a deprivation from physical activity survey to a selection of special-interest sports-related newsgroups. They found the three questionnaires administered to their Internet sample all displayed good to high internal consistencies, indicating that IMR can be used to gather reliable useful data. The study by Stanton (1998) mentioned above, which used company employees, found similar psychometric properties of a survey instrument administered to both Internet and non-Internet samples.

While the results above are encouraging, the issue of representativeness of Internet-accessed samples clearly continues to be a major concern amongst researchers who are thinking about, or actively engaged in, conducting Internet-based studies. This issue is essentially an empirical one and will only start to become clearer as a body of relevant research develops.[2] At the time of writing, only a handful of studies exist that systematically compare Internet and non-Internet samples.[3] Use of the Internet as a data-gathering tool is nevertheless becoming more and more widespread in social and behavioural research (for example, Bogaert, 1996; Browndyke et al., 1998; Buchanan, 2000; Coomber, 1997b; Goeritz and Schumacher, 2000; Sell, 1997; Senior et al., 1999; Stones and Perry, 1997). In practical terms, the researcher who is considering conducting IMR studies needs to be aware of the potential problems associated with sampling from the Internet, especially in cases where broad generalisability is desired. We take the studies outlined above as implying that this issue is not as problematic as has previously been suggested. However, other sources of evidence are relevant to this issue, and have been drawn upon by other researchers. Below we consider evidence from Internet-user surveys, and studies of Internet composition, before moving on to a discussion of the different Internet sampling procedures available.

To What Extent is Internet Sampling Problematic?

In addition to the above comments, we have two key points to make in relation to the claim that IMR is problematic because the Internet-user population is not representative of the population at large. First, many research questions do not require samples that are as closely representative of the 'population at large' as possible: for example, research that aims to focus on the characteristics of select groups, or that aims to provide an in-depth analysis of a small number of targeted individuals. Much research that adopts a more qualitative approach is concerned not with making broad generalisations, but with exploring and elucidating individual perspectives. In these cases concerns about sample representativeness do not pose a problem. Studies in cognitive psychology, concerned with low-level processes, may also be less likely to be sensitive to participants' biosocial or socioeconomic attributes (unlike, for example, studies of voting behaviour). So broad sample representativeness is certainly not always required.

Our second point is that in practice much reported research in the social sciences *is* based upon the use of select and homogeneous samples. It has been noted by several authors that psychological research studies have traditionally used students as research participants (for example, McNemar, 1946; Smart, 1966). This use of (mainly undergraduate psychology) students in psychological research still appears to be widespread. This is apparent merely by flicking through some of the major psychology journals. For example, the *Journal of Learning, Memory & Cognition*, Vol. 25, No. 1, January 1999 reports 14 studies, 12 of which recruited students as subjects (seven of these used psychology students). Of the remaining two studies, one used 'university members' and one used children from a particular primary school. The *Journal of Experimental Psychology: General*, Vol. 127, No. 4, December 1998 reports a total of 10 studies, 7 of which used student samples, 2 used 'university members', and 1 used second graders attending an after-school centre. Social psychology and sociology journals typically show less reliance on student research participants, drawing on other populations such as homeless adults, GPs and patients, police officers, nurses, and so on. However, even in these studies the samples used tend to be geographically homogeneous, for example drawn from a particular GP clinic, drop-in centre, or hospital ward.

Given this context, the Internet is extraordinary in that it affords the possibility of accessing far more diverse samples than has ever been practically possible before. The 100 million or so (e.g. MIDS, 1998) Internet users are located in geographically diverse locations all over the world and must, aside from any claims about inherent biases in terms of demographic or other characteristics, represent the most diverse and easily accessible group available to researchers in the behavioural and social sciences. The importance of this potential is even more apparent when we realise what it means for individual researchers, especially those working at smaller institutions that typically have fewer resources for supporting research than do larger, more established institutions. What the Internet offers these researchers is the potential to reach a vast number of research participants from all over the world cheaply and time-efficiently. In what follows we show why claims about biases in the Internet-user population are unfounded, and present evidence that demonstrates the vastness and diversity of this population.

Internet-User Surveys

The tendency is to support claims about biases in the characteristics of the Internet-user population by reference to data from 'WWW user surveys' (for example, Bordia, 1996; Sheehan and McMillian, 1999; Stanton, 1998; Szabo and Frenkl, 1996). Some of the surveys available are: CyberAtlas: The Web Marketer's Guide to Online Facts (*cyberatlas. Internet.com*), Cyber Dialogue (*www.cyberdialogue.com*), Stat Market (*www. statmarket.com*), and NUA Internet surveys (*www.nua.net/surveys*). The most comprehensive, longstanding, and detailed Internet-user survey reports come from the Graphics, Visualisation and Usability (GVU) Center, Georgia Institute of Technology. These reports have been published semi-annually since the first report in 1994 (Pitcow and Recker, 1994). The last publicly available GVU Internet user survey was the tenth, conducted in 1998. Georgia Tech's GVU Center has since teamed up with the Dupree College of Management to produce a commercially available survey.

Some of the main findings can be summarised (based on the GVU summary reports, available from *www.gvu.gatech.edu/user_surveys*). The ratio of male to female users has decreased across surveys, with the first survey reporting only 6 per cent of respondents female, but with this number steadily increasing until it appears to stabilise at around one-third of respondents female. The results that are most relevant to concerns about sample representativeness in Internet-based research are that in all surveys the respondents were primarily from the United States (somewhere between about 70 and 85 per cent in each survey), largely from education, computer, or professional occupations, and with an above-average mean income. Detailed figures can be found in the online GVU survey reports. The later reports give some interesting details concerning further categories: for example, the number of users who would describe themselves as having a disability; the most common platform used to access the Internet; whether the Internet is accessed primarily from home, work, or elsewhere; whether users pay for their Internet access themselves; and so on.

All these questions about the demographics, characteristics, and habits of Internet users are important in assessing the opportunities for Internet-based research. However, the assumptions made based on such data are premature. The typical assumption is that the Internet-user population is largely biased towards young North American males of above-average educational and socioeconomic status, and who work in computer-, education-, or technology-related fields. Aside from the fact that the later GVU surveys show only a two-thirds majority of male users, and in general suggest that the Internet-user population is becoming more and more representative of the population at large, there are strong methodological grounds for treating with extreme caution generalisations from the GVU survey results to the entire Internet-user population. For one thing, the surveys were only available in English, introducing an obvious immediate bias in the type of user who would respond. Further, the sampling procedures employed introduced additional bias. In the first GVU survey participants were recruited by officially announcing the survey on the *comp.infosystems.www* newsgroup and placing pointers on several other Web documents. Later surveys (for example, GVU, 1997) report recruiting respondents by posting announcements to Internet-related newsgroups, placing banners on high-exposure websites, posting announcements to a WWW-surveying mailing list, and placing announcements in popular media. We argue that while the latter technique is likely to produce a wider and more diverse sample of respondents than that employed in the first survey, even the more recent GVU surveys employ a sampling methodology that is clearly biased towards selecting a particular type of Internet user.

Essentially, the GVU surveys placed their announcements in locations where overwhelmingly the main viewers would be those interested in the World Wide Web in itself, rather than interested in that which is available over the Web. This is an important distinction because it means a substantial number of the (self-selecting) group who responded to these surveys were interested in issues like the demographics of the Web, or in the most popular software used to access the Web, rather than, for instance, twentieth-century Irish literature.

Moreover, the number of GVU survey respondents is small when considered in relation to the entire Internet-user population. The executive summary of the seventh survey, for example, states: 'The GVU's Seventh WWW User Survey, which was conducted April 10 through May 10 1997, received over 87,000 responses from 19,970 respondents. If we assume the current WWW user population to be around 30 million, then one out of every 1,500 users responded to the Seventh Survey' (GVU, 1997). Coupled with the bias towards selecting the more technologically proficient user who is interested in WWW- and computer-related issues, and who speaks English, we consider this good grounds for rejecting any claims that the GVU survey statistics are representative of the whole Internet-user population. The GVU survey team are explicit in highlighting this point, noting that a bias exists in the 'experience, intensity of usage, and skill sets of the users' who responded to their surveys (GVU, 1997). Yet such methodological considerations are typically overlooked by authors who warn us about the skewed demographics of the Internet-user population.

Internet composition

In our view one of the most important and reliable sources of information in gaining a picture of the size and diversity of the Internet-user population comes from analyses of Internet composition. The most respected analysis of Internet composition grew out of Mark Lottor's semi-annual reports of the number of Internet-accessible hosts (Lottor, 1992). The number of such hosts accessible in July 1995 was 6.6 million. In January 1996 this figure rose to 9.5 million. The most recent figure at the time of writing stands at 147 million (Internet software consortium, *www.isc.org/*, January 2002). In order to assess what this means in terms of the number of Internet users and their locations world-wide, we need to take into account some considerations concerning computer network configurations. A popular configuration for an Internet-accessible site has been to have a single 'server' (host) that acts as the point of access to the external world, and a greater number of computers networked to that host machine. This configuration is still widely used. As Lottor (1996) points out, no one can construct a reliable estimate of the number of actual Internet users. Based on the aforementioned configuration it would certainly be a conservative estimate to assume one user for each host; a more reliable estimate may be best constructed by polling the 'poorer' sites to construct an average number of computers networked to a given host, and number of users per given computer.

However, more recent developments have further complicated the issue. While the configuration described above was once predominant, nowadays another common configuration is to have a local network of PCs each with their own IP (Internet Protocol, described in Chapter 4) address, which means that each PC will appear as a separate host. However, many PCs will have multiple users – universities, for example, maintain computer rooms in which each machine serves a large number of users. In this case, each apparent host address would support a large number of users. Further complications arise from the use of 'firewalls'[4] and 'proxies',[5] which may make all hosts in a given organisation appear as one from the outside. Also, very large numbers of users and organisations now use dialup (in which the user connects to a server using the public telephone network, via a modem), where the number of apparent hosts is again smaller than the number of actual ones, due to dynamic IP addressing. In this case the ISP (Internet Service Provider) has a pool of IP addresses that are allocated to computers as they connect, and deallocated when they hang up. Thus the number of actual hosts hugely exceeds the size of the namespace allocated to the ISP, and the actual hosts change on a minute-to-minute basis. Additional complications arise because many people may use more than one computer, and many may have accounts with several free ISPs. In this case the same person may appear as several users, based on counting Internet host addresses.

All the above considerations complicate the reliability of estimates of the number of actual Internet users. Essentially, knowledge of popular network configurations, as well as patterns of usage, are important in estimating the size of the Internet-user population. How many people use multi-user systems? How many hosts are family PCs with multiple users, or machines in cybercafés or public terminal rooms? How many machines are solely used by a given individual? How many individuals use more than one host address? Some idea of the answers to these questions is necessary in estimating the actual number of Internet users. Given that universities, colleges, public libraries, hospitals, Internet cafés, and a large number of other organisations make use of configurations in which a number of computers are used by a far greater number of users, we would safely bet that the number of actual users vastly exceeds the number of apparent hosts. Of course, there are also many cases in which individuals have exclusive access to their own computer: university lecturers, researchers, administrative staff, and so on. However, overall we feel confident in estimating that the number of multiple users per host far outweighs the number of multiple hosts per user. At the time of writing, recent estimates of the Internet-user population have suggested figures exceeding the 500 million mark (for example, Nva Ltd, *www.nva.ie/surveys/how-many-online/world.html* (accessed April 2002); Computer Industry Almanac Inc., *www.c-i-a.com/pr032102.htm* (accessed April 2002)). Given the figures reported above on the number of Internet-accessible hosts (147 million, January 2002), we would consider this figure to be a rather conservative current estimate.

The diversity of the Internet-accessible population is spoken for, in part, by the number of international 'entities' (roughly corresponding to nations) that are deemed to have widespread international Internet access. In one of the most comprehensive analyses to date (Landweber, 1997) there were 195 entities with international network connectivity. Given the difficulty of thinking of so many entities, it seems worth listing some of them to give an impression of the diversity this entails:

Algeria, Antarctica, Argentina, Armenia, Australia, Austria, Azerbaijan, Bangladesh, Barbados, Belarus, Belgium, Belize, Bermuda, Bolivia, Brazil, Bulgaria, Burkina, Faso (formerly Upper Volta), Cameroon, Canada, Chile, China, Colombia, Democratic Republic of Congo, Costa Rica, Côte d'Ivoire, Croatia, Cuba, Cyprus, Czech Republic, Denmark, Dominican Republic, Ecuador, Egypt, Estonia, Faroe Islands, Fiji, Finland, France, Georgia, Germany, Greece, Greenland, Guam, Hong Kong, Hungary, Iceland, India, Indonesia, Iran, Ireland, Israel, Italy, Jamaica, Japan, Kazakhstan, South Korea, Kyrgyz Republic, Kuwait, Latvia, Lebanon, Liechtenstein, Lithuania, Luxembourg, Macau (Ao-me'n), Madagascar, Malaysia, Mali, Mexico, Moldova, Monaco, Morocco, Mozambique, Namibia, Netherlands, New Caledonia, New Zealand, Nicaragua, Niger, Nigeria, Norway, Pakistan, Panama, Peru, Philippines, Poland, Portugal, Puerto Rico, Réunion, Romania, Russian Federation, Saudi Arabia, Senegal, Singapore, Slovakia, Slovenia, South Africa, Spain, Sri Lanka, Svalbard and Jan Mayen Islands, Sweden, Switzerland, Taiwan, Thailand, Tunisia, Turkey, Ukraine, United Kingdom, United States, Uruguay, Uzbekistan, Venezuela, Vietnam (Socialist Republic), and Zambia.

Once this list is reflected upon it becomes rather evident that the 20,000 or so distinct respondents to the GVU surveys cannot be representative of the full population of Internet users.

We hope that the above discussion has demonstrated several key points in relation to Internet-accessed samples. First, data from Internet-user surveys should not be taken as an accurate representation of the characteristics of Internet users in general. Second, information concerning Internet composition is valuable in gaining a picture of the size and diversity of the Internet-user population, especially given the sampling problems associated with Internet-user surveys. Third, estimating the size of the Internet-user population is by no means a simple matter. And finally, the evidence available suggests that the total number of Internet users world-wide well exceeds the 500 million mark, and represents a far more diverse segment of the population than has been suggested.

We do not deny that certain groups have been, and still are, largely excluded from the Internet-user population (for example, those disinterested in computer technology, those unable to afford Internet access).[6] Researchers interested in these groups will clearly not find the Internet useful as a primary research tool. However, this does not detract from the fact that the Internet provides enormous potential for reaching a vast number of research participants from diverse locations all over the world. In many instances the Internet may open up opportunities for researchers to contact individuals who would otherwise be practically inaccessible.

Furthermore, the evidence suggests that the Internet-user population is continuing to expand at a great rate. The Internet, and particularly the World Wide Web, appears to be becoming more and more a part of everyday life. We predict that this trend will continue, and that the number of non-specialist Internet users who use the Internet primarily for recreational or consumer purposes will continue to grow. Biases clearly exist. For example, North American users who access the Internet from home via their phone line are likely to spend more time online than are British users, due to differences in local call tolls (American local calls are free whereas in Britain local calls are billed depending on call length, though a number of British telephone companies are now offering free Internet calls for a moderate fixed monthly fee).

Services are also becoming available that allow people to access email and Internet via their television sets. The latest development, at time of writing, is Internet access via a mobile phone. Such developments will no doubt widen Internet access for the recreational as well as business user.

Internet Sampling Methodologies

So far we have argued that the Internet provides great potential for accessing research participants. We now outline the types of sampling procedures that are available using the Internet, and discuss the advantages and problems associated with these techniques.

Volunteer Samples

Internet research to date is based overwhelmingly on the use of volunteer participants. This is evident in published papers (for example,

Browndyke et al., 1998; Buchanan and Smith, 1999a; Hewson, 1994; Krantz et al., 1997; Smith and Leigh, 1997; Szabo et al., 1996) and World Wide Web sites dedicated to the cataloguing of ongoing Internet-based research studies (for example, Web Experimental Psychology Lab: *www.psych.unizh.ch/genpsy/Ulf/Lab/WebExpPsyLab.html*; American Psychological Society – Psychological Research on the Net: *psych.hanover.edu/APS/exponnet.html*). The standard technique uses a non-probabilistic sampling methodology that obtains volunteer participants. Two general approaches are popular. One is to place on web sites announcements that advertise the study and provide instructions on how to take part (for example, Krantz et al., 1997; Senior and Smith, 1999). This method relies on Internet users coming across the announcements as they browse the World Wide Web and making an active decision to volunteer to take part in the study. There are a range of possibilities for how to carry out the study itself, such as directing the user to a particular web site that executes a program,[7] asking the user to use FTP (File Transfer Protocol, discussed in Chapter 4) to obtain study materials, or asking him or her to communicate with the researcher by email to receive materials or further instructions.

A second approach is to post announcements to a selection of newsgroups[8] (for example, Browndyke et al., 1998; Buchanan and Smith, 1999a). This is similar to the previous method but gives the researcher more control over the type of user who is likely to see the announcements since it is possible to target particular specific-interest newsgroups, as well as restrict distribution to a specific location (for example, a particular country, as explained in Chapter 4). This standard current methodology raises two problems however: the use of non-probabilistic sampling; and the use of volunteer participants.

Non-probabilistic sampling raises the concern of generalisability. As noted in relation to the GVU Internet-user surveys, posting announcements to particular newsgroups or web sites is likely to select a particular type of user. In the case of the GVU surveys the bias was towards selecting the more experienced and frequent North American Internet user with a particular interest in WWW-related issues. Clearly the generalisability of data is limited in cases where such biases are likely to exist. However, we do not consider this a major problem for Internet-based research. For one thing, there are many research questions where broad generalisability of data is not what is required (as mentioned previously).

Further, the use of non-probabilistic samples in social scientific research is already widespread. Numerous reported studies rely on opportunistic sampling techniques, often leading to samples consisting entirely of undergraduate students (as discussed earlier).[9] No doubt this situation is largely dictated by financial and practical constraints. However, given this context, the Internet presents a valuable new tool that can greatly enhance opportunities for accessing larger and more diverse samples, giving researchers more scope for moving beyond samples of undergraduate students, university members, and other small homogeneous groups. This potential still needs to be realised. A large number of the studies that appear online today are posted on sites specifically dedicated to Internet-based research, and thus will capture an audience who have a special interest in this topic. Though these sites may seem an obvious starting place for researchers developing Internet-based research projects to recruit participants, we stress the importance of carefully considering the associated sampling biases. Supplementing with postings to a range of other WWW sites or newsgroups can help reduce such biases.

The reliance on volunteer participants in IMR is more worrying, for several reasons. The issue is not new and there is a large body of literature that discusses possible biases involved in using volunteers as research participants. For example, volunteers have been found to differ from non-volunteers on personality variables (for example, Bogaert, 1996; Coye, 1985; Dollinger and Frederick, 1993) and sexual behaviour and attitudes (for example, Morokoff, 1986; Strassberg and Kristi, 1995). Any such characteristics that are found to distinguish volunteer participants from non-volunteers must be taken into account, and may well limit the generalisability of results, depending on the particular research question.

A further problem associated with the use of volunteer participants is that it becomes very difficult to get an idea of the sampling frame. How does the researcher know how many people saw the announcement? What types of people saw the announcement? Without this information it is impossible to assess the extent to which the sampling procedure introduced bias. For example, did a larger proportion of males than females who saw the announcement volunteer to take part? Or were those who responded people with a particular interest in the research area? For this reason traditional social science research has avoided the use of 'true volunteers'. Yet in Internet-mediated research this methodology is by far the most widely used. This must be largely due to the ability of this method to generate large numbers of participants with minimal researcher effort. Indeed, if postings are sent to a wide range of WWW sites and newsgroups, then the samples obtained can be very large and diverse. But unless we can ensure validity of data, and generalisability where required, access to such large samples is of little use.

The problems associated with the use of volunteer samples in IMR have been noted by researchers in the field, and some solutions have been suggested (Strauss, 1996). One approach has been to rely on minimising sampling bias by obtaining extremely large samples. Another has been to try to estimate the number of users who have seen the study announcement by counting the number of hits to the web site(s) where it has been advertised during the exposure period. Such methods may be useful as rough guidelines for helping to minimise sampling bias, and to get some idea of response rates, for the researcher who is already involved in carrying out large-scale Internet-mediated research. However, in order to be able to assess the validity of IMR sampling procedures more clearly, a more structured approach is needed. The approach we recommended earlier in this chapter is to validate data from Internet samples through comparison with non-Internet samples. As noted, several authors have already taken such an approach, with promising results (Buchanan and Smith, 1999a; Smith and Leigh, 1997).

Potential for Accessing Non-Volunteer Samples

Another likely reason for the widespread use of volunteer participants in IMR is that contacting individuals directly via the Internet has been considered more problematic than in traditional research. Using traditional methods it is often fairly easy directly to contact students, members of the public, patients, professionals, home-owners, and so on, by locating individuals and sending direct individual requests. This may be done face-to-face, as when a researcher asks a group of students in a lecture to take part in a study, or through a postal address or telephone number. In this way a record of all requests for participation can be maintained, allowing comparison of respondents and non-respondents, and assessment of non-response rate and non-response bias.

To contact individuals directly via the Internet requires locating their personal email addresses. This is certainly possible. The researcher who plans to attend a lecture session in order to administer a research procedure may instead obtain a list of the email addresses of all students in that class, and send a request for participation via this medium. In some cases it may be possible to obtain very large lists of email addresses through some organisation or other source. Indeed, lists with millions of email addresses are routinely on offer for a moderate fee (the email advertisements we have been sent offering such lists cost from around $50–$200 or £35–£140). While these lists may be of use for some researchers involved in large-scale survey research, many researchers will not require such large populations. Further, the lack of control over (and lack of knowledge of) the sampling frame makes this approach unattractive, even in cases where the research budget would allow it. Knowing when and where participants' email addresses were harvested from is important,[10] and alternative approaches to compiling lists of email addresses (outlined later) are recommended. Various issues arise in relation to the approach of contacting individuals via email. How can we be sure that the accounts mailed are not dormant and that the request has been read?[11] Is it ethical to send participation requests to individuals' mailboxes (or is it an invasion of privacy)? How does the researcher avoid being accused of 'spamming' (a term used to refer to the posting of unwanted nuisance mail to individuals' mailboxes)?[12] The practical and methodological issues are taken up further in later chapters. Ethical guidelines with respect to IMR will be discussed below, though we do not consider the sending of personal email requests to be problematic as long as certain criteria are met.

Another problem with the approach of contacting potential participants directly by email is that the scope for estimating non-response bias effects can be limited, due to the fact that email addresses themselves convey very little information about characteristics such as age, sex, nationality, and so on. We may be able to guess from his or her email address that a user is most likely from a particular country, or works in a certain subject area or organisation, but this information is unreliable and limited. Thus while allowing an assessment of non-response rates (putting aside the problem of dormant email accounts), such email-based sampling procedures do not automatically allow for assessment of non-response bias. Of course in many instances information concerning demographic and biosocial characteristics may also be available alongside users' email addresses, thus overcoming this problem.

Another approach is to contact individuals and ask them to administer the study materials on the researcher's behalf. This approach was adopted by Hewson and Vogel (1994) in a reasoning study. They contacted teachers through SchoolNet (in addition to posting calls to newsgroups), an electronic network of Canadian schools, and asked if they would be willing to administer the test materials to their students? By this method a sample of 52 participants was generated. This procedure presents a further alternative to the dominant approach and avoids the use of true volunteers; however, it requires the cooperation of a third party, and also raises issues relating to reduced researcher control.

Further possibilities are available. Bordia (1996) has reported an observational study of verbal interaction and rumour transmission using a BITNET discussion group, and argues for the ethical acceptability of this approach (subscribers were not aware their postings were being used). A similar study was carried out by Herring et al. (1998) to look at gender differences in online communication. Discourse analysis may be carried out using the archives from discussion groups, advertisements, or other documents available on the Internet. If confidentiality is ensured, and given that authors publish such documents with the knowledge that they are publicly available, we do not consider this approach to raise any serious ethical problems, though this statement is bound to raise controversy.

The above examples demonstrate that although most IMR makes use of procedures that generate volunteer samples, this is by no means the only option available. Various procedures are possible that avoid the use of volunteer participants, and given the problems outlined in relation to volunteer samples we would urge readers to consider these alternatives carefully. Of course, the nature of the research question, as well as practical considerations, will influence the choices made.

Possibilities for Probabilistic Sampling

Probabilistic sampling has been considered the ideal within the behavioural and social sciences (Smith, 1975). In practice, much research carried out does not achieve true probabilistic sampling. In relation to IMR the scope for probabilistic sampling is also fairly limited, the point being that there is currently no central register of all Internet users. It may be possible to attain probability samples of smaller populations, such as students at a particular university, as long as enumeration of all members of the population is possible. Moving beyond the academic population, it may be feasible to access all users registered with a particular Internet Service Provider, online banking service, or other enumerable group, though issues relating to security and confidentiality may well restrict such access. But for many research issues and target populations such enumeration will not be possible. News servers, for example, do not generally hold a list of all subscribers and therefore it would not be possible to obtain a list of all readers of a particular newsgroup. Lists of subscribers are available for mailing lists, but there are complications. Some apparent subscribers may in fact be aliases of other mailing lists, which would lead to underestimating the actual number of subscribers.

The scope for Internet-based probability sampling requires further exploration. We are aware of a few research studies to date that have attempted to use techniques that at least approximate probability sampling. One approach is to select randomly from a list of USENET groups, and then obtain email addresses by sampling randomly from postings to these groups over a certain period. Other Internet outlets where email addresses are posted (such as chat forums and bulletin boards) can be used in a similar manner. A number of researchers have used this type of approach (for example, Penkoff et al., 1996; Swoboda et al., 1997; Witmer et al., 1999). Another approach is to select randomly from visitors to a particular web site. Dahlen (1998) has piloted this approach by implementing a program (using JavaScript, which is described in later chapters) to keep track of all visitors to a particular high-traffic web site, and contact every 200th visitor via a pop-up box requesting participation. The problem of multiple requests being made to users who visited the site more than once was controlled by keeping track of visitors by using 'cookies' (these place a 'tag' in the user's browser and are then recognised on multiple visits). Recording whether the users declined or participated allowed measurement of response rate. A weakness of this methodology is that it obtains a probability sample of the browsers that visit the web site, not users, and we cannot assume a one-to-one correspondence between the two.[13] Also, while visitors to the web site comprise the known sampling frame, the characteristics of members of this frame will be largely unknown.

For some research questions and goals obtaining a probability sample may be practical and appropriate. For others it may not be possible, or necessary. But the use of non-probability samples is not atypical in social and behavioural research, and this methodology poses no particular problems for IMR. Even though the scope for probability sampling in IMR has been considered fairly limited, the above procedures show that it is to some extent possible, and opportunities may well be enhanced by future technological developments and further piloting of procedures.

Generating Data: Possibilities in Internet-Mediated Research

Once research participants have been recruited, data need to be collected. Though the features of the Internet put some limitations on the types of research methodologies that can be employed, a wide range of tools, instruments, techniques, and research domains can be adapted. We outline the advantages of implementing various procedures in an Internet medium. We also discuss the caveats and offer solutions where possible.[14] Further, and perhaps more importantly, the Internet opens up new possibilities for conducting research – ones that take us beyond the scope of traditional methods. We highlight these possibilities.

Questionnaires

The questionnaire is the most obvious, easily adaptable tool for use in Internet-mediated research, and it is certainly the most widely used to date (for example, Browndyke et al., 1998; Coomber, 1997b; Goeritz and Schumacher, 2000; Stones and Perry, 1997). To administer a questionnaire via email is very easy and requires only a minimal level of technical competency (see case study 1, Chapter 7). With a little more expertise (or at least the assistance of a support technician) the researcher can administer the questionnaire by placing it on a web site, creating even less work once the site has been constructed since all that remains to be done is sit and wait for data to come in[15] (though, as discussed in later chapters, we recommend controlling access to a Web-based survey, rather than allowing participation by anyone who happens to stumble across the survey online). The range of research questions and approaches that a questionnaire methodology supports is vast. Marketing researchers make extensive use of survey questionnaires to gather data on consumer attitudes, preferences, and behaviours. Surveys (including questionnaires and interviews) are commonly used in sociological research, political science, and psychology. Psychologists make use of attitude scales and psychometric tests that are administered in questionnaire format. In fact, the use of survey-based techniques within the social sciences has been so widespread that survey research has come to be virtually synonymous with social scientific research (Smith, 1975). Essentially, any technique that involves presenting research participants with a set of verbal questions requiring verbal responses can be easily implemented via the Internet, thus making IMR immediately broad in its scope for supporting a range of research topics.

What are the advantages of using the Internet as a tool for administering questionnaires, as compared with traditional methods? There are several. First, the Internet can dramatically increase the time- and cost-efficiency of a piece of research. Distribution of a questionnaire via the Internet reduces both the time and costs associated with producing numerous hard copies of materials, distribution and data collection (for example, postage or staffing costs), and converting data into a format ready for analysis. In traditional methodologies constraints on these resources can limit the number of research participants available. However, using an IMR approach, once the file containing the questionnaire has been created, it can be quickly and easily administered to any number of research participants with no further expense than the standard Internet connection charges (assuming these are paid anyway by the researcher's institution). Data collection is facilitated since responses come back in electronic format and can be directed straight to an appropriate file, even coded and sorted. This ability of IMR to greatly reduce the timescale and cost of a piece of research can enable projects that are not yet funded, such as a preliminary study for use in a funding application, or, for projects that do have funding, can allow much larger data sets to be collected.

A second advantage of IMR is that it enables access to a vast and diverse group of potential research participants. Traditional methods, even postal administered surveys, do not have the same capacity for accessing such large numbers of people from all over the world. This collapsing of geographical boundaries in IMR enhances the possibilities for cross-cultural research, which in many cases may otherwise be unfeasible due to time or funding constraints. Further advantages of an Internet-mediated approach to questionnaire-based research can be speculated upon, though these speculations demand empirical investigation. From the research participants' point of view an Internet-administered questionnaire may be more appealing, for several reasons. First there is the novelty value of responding to an Internet-based study, which may enhance its appeal to potential participants. Further, participants are able to complete the whole process – receiving materials, giving responses, posting back to the researcher – from the comfort of their own home and at a time that suits them. Such factors may help to enhance response rates compared with, for example, postal surveys. The types of factors that enhance or reduce response rates to Internet-administered questionnaires need to be explored (though some existing research is discussed in Chapter 5).

The above considerations make the idea of an Internet-based approach to primary research very attractive. However, in any piece of research, ensuring both reliability and validity of data is of prime importance. There are features of IMR that make data validity an issue. In general, Internet-based procedures are likely to reduce the level of researcher control and involvement. Thus when materials are administered via a computer terminal, rather than in person, the researcher is less able to judge the extent to which responses are sincere and genuine, the conditions under which the questionnaire was answered, the state of participants at the time of participation (for example, intoxicated, distracted, and so on), and the identity of participants. The possibility of fraudulent responses means that asking participants for details of these factors may not lead to accurate information. The extent to which this lack of direct control may pose a problem for IMR needs to be explored, though, as mentioned earlier, some studies have already indicated that Internet-based procedures give results comparable to non-Internet procedures. This suggests that these issues may not pose a major problem, and that in general we may assume our participants are giving genuine and accurate responses, especially if we follow the guidelines in the following chapters for maximising researcher control and minimising the potential for malicious and fraudulent replies.[16] Another factor that can reduce levels of researcher control is system diversity.[17] This issue is more likely to be a problem for designs that go beyond purely text-based materials, as will be discussed in the relevant sections below.

Traditional methods have administered questionnaires via post, telephone, or face-to-face. An Internet-administered questionnaire may be seen as sharing more with the first of these approaches, in that reduced control is traded for cost- and time-efficiency. However, an Internet-based approach allows even greater numbers of participants to be contacted with less time and cost expenditure. Further, the Internet questionnaire, like the postal questionnaire, allows anonymity of both researcher and participant. This may help reduce biases associated with attributes such as sex, age, nationality, and so on, as well as perhaps encouraging candidness, increasing response rates, and reducing demand characteristics. Increased accuracy due to the removal of researcher transcription of verbal responses is another advantage of postal questionnaires over telephone and face-to-face methods, and is also a feature shared by Internet administrations. While the Internet shares and enhances all the above outlined benefits of postal questionnaires, it also has the additional feature of allowing greater levels of interactivity, as shall now be discussed.

Interviews

The scope for interactive communication afforded by the Internet means it can be used to conduct interviews yet, unlike any existing method, complete anonymity can be maintained. Interviewer and interviewee need not know anything about each other's identity or biosocial attributes. This makes the Internet unique as a tool for conducting interviews and opens up new possibilities. On the other hand, the flexibility of an Internet interview, as well as the scope for making use of body language and other non-verbal information, is reduced. Essentially, it is down to the individual researcher to decide whether an Internet methodology will provide a better alternative to more traditional interview techniques for his or her particular research question. The type of situation where an Internet methodology could prove extremely advantageous is when a researcher is looking at 'rare cases', or individuals who are otherwise difficult to locate. Newsgroups can be used to locate individuals with common interests from all over the world. Another example is research that addresses sensitive topics; it may be easier to conduct such research using the Internet due to the more anonymous nature of the interaction. Research that needs to be conducted on a tight budget, or in a short space of time, may also benefit due to the features of IMR outlined previously.

How could an Internet-based interview be conducted? Most simply, an interview may be conducted by email. The researcher can send a set of questions to the participant, who can then respond to these simply by posting back a reply email. This interaction can be ongoing and thus allow for follow-up questions, clarification of ambiguities, and so on. Compared with traditional interview methods the email interview may be less spontaneous and flowing, but it allows respondents to answer in their own time, as and when it is convenient for them. This may encourage more detailed and carefully considered answers. Further, respondents may be more accurate in answering factual questions since they are able to go and check information, and this may enhance the validity and quality of data obtained.

While email interviews may be useful for a large number of research questions, in some situations a more continuous ongoing interaction might be sought. This is possible via the Internet using interactive chat facilities (see Chapter 4 for further details of the tools available). In short, such facilities allow two or more individuals to interact by typing concurrently at their computer screens, allowing a 'conversation' to be conducted. Some readers may be familiar with this procedure through visiting online 'chat rooms'. This chat facility can easily be adapted for the purpose of conducting an online interview; the interviewer and interviewee simply need to arrange a time to log on and carry out the interview online. The benefits of such an approach include those already outlined as general advantages of IMR: wider access to participants, automatic logging of data, reduced costs. Compared with an email interview, an online chat allows a more flowing communication, closer to traditional methods. However, it loses the potential benefits of allowing participants more freedom to respond at their leisure, as well as placing more demands on the researcher's own time.

Both email and chat-based approaches to interviewing differ from traditional methods, most starkly in that there is little scope for using extra-linguistic cues in online interactions. Also, as mentioned above, online interactions can be completely anonymous. The effects of such factors constitute an area of research in itself. Whether these features will prove to be advantages or disadvantages in an IMR approach to interviewing remains to be clarified by future research, and as always will no doubt depend on the particular research question at hand. Finally, the potential for using video and sound in Internet communications is developing, and may open further possibilities for conducting Internet-based interview research.[18]

Observation Studies

Observational techniques are used in a wide variety of contexts. Many people will associate observational research with studies in which the researcher acts as a passive observer of human (or animal) behaviour in a naturalistic setting. Alternatives to this prototypical model are participant observation, in which the researcher actively engages in interaction with those being observed, and observation in the laboratory, which may or may not use an experimental approach. The scope for observational research on the Internet is somewhat restricted, essentially being limited to what may be called 'indirect observation', by which we mean observation of the traces of behaviour (such as archived postings to newsgroups) as opposed to observations of behaviour in real time and close proximity.[19] In this sense all Internet observation will be indirect. Further, the primary form of communication on the Internet is language-based. However, this makes the Internet ideal for linguistic observation studies.

Naturalistic studies can be conducted that examine the nature of Internet-based communication itself (for example, Bordia, 1996; Herring et al., 1998). Other situations may be constructed that examine linguistic behaviour in particular contexts or settings manipulated by the researcher. The general advantages of IMR apply, but a further advantage of linguistic observation on the Internet is the non-intrusiveness of the observation (Bordia, 1996). Since the researcher is able to locate suitable data from archives (of discussion group postings, and so on), he or she does not need to be present during the data-generation phase. This is true for any observational study conducted via the Internet, since it is always possible to log the behaviour of the user at the keyboard. Bordia (1996) notes that this opens up opportunities that were previously unavailable and could be important in being able to remove observer presence biases. In addition, being able to search archives makes it more efficient for the researcher to locate appropriate data without, for example, wasting time recording material that may after all turn out to be irrelevant to the research topic. The distinct features of Internet-based verbal communication make generalisability beyond this domain unwarranted, but the rapid growth of the Internet has generated a whole new research area in Internet communication itself.

Beyond linguistic observation the Internet offers opportunities for observing non-linguistic aspects of behaviour. A range of approaches are conceivable, for example presenting participants with problem-solving or decision-making tasks, using simulations to observe behaviour in certain hypothetical situations, constructing games (for example, to look at gambling behaviour), or using role-play (see Smith, 1975, for a discussion of the merits and limitations of simulation and gaming approaches). In cases where direct proximal interaction is not essential, such approaches can be implemented by means of interaction with a program, or other participants, via a computer terminal, and a log of the participants' behaviour can be obtained. Essentially, almost any piece of research that could be implemented offline using a computer program can also be implemented online over the Internet (though a few qualifications to this are outlined in the following section). The use of Netcams is also a future possibility, one which could provide a good approximation to direct proximal observation that goes beyond observation of typed responses. However, this possibility will depend on technological advances to improve the picture and sound quality of Netcams. At the time of writing the use of Netcams for anything like observation of body language, or real-time interaction is seriously limited by bandwidth[20] constraints, and the fact that most Internet users do not actually have access to a Netcam. We know of no IMR that has attempted to use Netcams.

Experiments

While a large body of primary research being conducted on the Internet involves questionnaire and survey-based research, there are also a substantial number of studies that employ an experimental methodology (many can be found at *www.psych.unizh.ch/genpsy/Ulf/Lab/WebExpPsyLab.html*). In an experimental design the researcher manipulates the independent variable(s) in order to measure the effect on the dependent variable(s), participants being randomly assigned to each of the experimental conditions. Though recent accounts have challenged the predominance of the experimental method in psychological research, and suggested that psychology is undergoing a paradigm shift towards emphasis on more qualitative approaches (Smith et al., 1995), the experiment is probably still the most widely used research technique in psychology. Experiments are used to study a wide range of issues across many areas of psychology and employing a range of techniques, procedures, and instruments. The experimental method is also used in the other social sciences, though to a lesser degree. Here we identify four general types of commonly used experimental procedure and assess the scope for implementing these in IMR. First are experiments that present static printed materials (for example, printed text or graphics); second are those that make use of non-printed materials (for example, video or sound); third are reaction-time experiments; and fourth are experiments that involve some form of interpersonal interaction.

The first type of experiment is readily adaptable to an Internet medium. As discussed in relation to questionnaire and survey research, it is easy to create a file that presents text. Graphics can also be presented with little technical expertise (Senior et al., 1999, conducted a World Wide Web experiment that presented schematic faces). As noted in relation to questionnaire studies, the researcher may choose to send the files to participants by email or place them on a web page. In many cases the experimental manipulation will be based upon differences in the materials presented, which means that the researcher simply needs to send different materials to different participants. In other cases (quasi-experimental designs) it will be the comparison of different groups based on participant characteristics that is of interest. Again such designs are easy to implement. Other manipulations may involve some participants having to take part in a further task or procedure prior to, or in between, measurements. To the extent that these procedures involve presentation of text- or graphics-based materials, they pose no problem for implementation via the Internet. The usual benefits of IMR make implementation of this type of study on the Internet an attractive option. However, particular care must be taken to ensure that presentation format of materials is the same for all participants. Problems can arise, for example, when viewing an HTML (HyperText Mark-up Language, described in Chapter 4) file using different browsers, such as Netscape Navigator and Internet Explorer. Such uncontrolled variations can threaten data validity. However, it is possible to construct HTML files so that presentation formats will remain constant. The key point here is to make sure that maximal control over such variations is maintained, and to test-run experimental materials before making them available to participants. Detailed solutions are given in the next chapter.

Another issue relates to file size and download time – larger files will take longer to download, which could cause participants to give up on the experiment before completion. This will be more of a problem for graphics than text files, and again requires a pre-experiment testing phase to ensure that download times are not excessive. Once more, solutions are outlined in the next chapter.

The issue of download times and different user platforms (that is, different hardware) is more of a problem for the second type of experiment, which uses sound- or video-based materials. Most computer users will have the facilities to play sound and video clips so it is certainly possible to present materials of this type. However, using sound and video files that are too large could lead to delays during the experimental procedure as files are downloaded from the server to the user's machine. It is therefore important to keep files to a manageable size, and this will impose some limitations on the type of materials that can reasonably be presented. In addition, since different users will be using different machines there may well be slight variations in the way materials appear to participants. Slower machines will lead to lower-quality playback. Faster machines will be able to cope with larger files and will result in better quality. This technological issue must be carefully considered when conducting such studies. One possible solution would be to make sure the materials will run at an optimum level on the slowest machines. Another option would be to specify the minimum hardware requirements needed to run the experiment adequately, and aim to ensure that participants adhere to these (further possibilities are explored in Chapter 4). While these measures impose constraints on the experiments that can be conducted, they are important in ensuring data validity. Further, as computer technology continues to develop at a rapid pace, the scope for IMR that utilises multimedia presentations continues to broaden. Currently the types of research that may benefit from the use of sound- and video-based presentation are those that require relatively small and easily downloadable files: for example, psycholinguistic studies concerned with speech recognition, or musical perception studies, both of which may be able to use manageable-sized sound clips.

Reaction-time experiments, the third type of experiments to be considered here, demand precise and accurate measurement (typically to the level of a millisecond). In a traditional setting this is possible by getting the participant to interact with a computer program that can present materials and measure reaction times to this level of precision. However, transporting this methodology to an Internet medium, raises problems, which arise as a result of different user platforms and Internet connection speeds. If participants are asked to log on to an Internet site and interact with a program, then factors such as the user's modem speed and the amount of network traffic will create variations that will lead to inaccuracies in measurement. However, adopting a procedure whereby the program is actually downloaded onto the user's machine and run off-line could provide a solution to this, in which case reaction-time experiments may be possible in IMR, though further research is needed to clarify the reliability of such methods. At the time of writing we could find no reports of IMR that attempted to make precise timing measurements.

The final type of experiment we consider involves interaction between participants. This is possible in an Internet medium using facilities such as interactive chat, mentioned earlier, which allows several users to interact at the same time. Some studies may not find this useful given the limited nature of the interaction: it is purely language-based and does not allow the use of extra-linguistic information (body-language, intonation, and so on). However, the nature of Internet interaction itself constitutes a whole new area of research. For example, Internet users have developed a system of symbolic representations to convey prosodic information (for example, upper case means 'shouting') and facial expressions (for example, :-) means a smile). This system has become quite elaborate and widespread and provides the researcher studying linguistic interaction on the Internet with richer data. In addition to studies of linguistic interaction in IMR further possibilities are available. Using multi-user environments it would be possible for several participants to engage mutually in some kind of task, or game, in which behaviour beyond linguistic communication could be recorded: for example, moving around in a dynamic environment, or engaging in some kind of role play. This extends the possibilities for interactive experiments in IMR beyond those that are purely linguistic. Video cameras and microphones linked up to the Internet may create further possibilities, though currently the technology available for this is limited.

In this section we have outlined a range of possibilities for gathering data via the Internet, highlighting the types of traditional research techniques that may be implemented and the advantages and disadvantages of adapting these methodologies to an IMR approach. The next chapter gives a more detailed account of the tools available for use in IMR, and the ways in which these can be used to support particular methodologies. Chapter 5 then describes how to design and implement a World Wide Web survey. Many of the issues highlighted in the current chapter are addressed in more detail in Chapters 4 and 5, with specific solutions and procedures recommended. But first we summarise the general advantages of IMR and consider ethical issues in such research.

General Advantages of Internet-Mediated Primary Research: When and Why Would it be Better to Conduct a Study via the Internet?

The general advantages of conducting a study via the Internet have been outlined. These are cost- and time-efficiency and access to a large and diverse population of potential participants. These features may be particularly important for smaller institutions that have little time and money available for research, and therefore IMR is a very appealing option for them. However, some issues which may threaten data validity have also been outlined. These include sample bias and lack of researcher control. The first of these issues has been addressed and we hope the reader is convinced by our arguments that sampling bias does not pose a major problem for Internet-based research if given careful consideration, and effective procedures are implemented. The issue of researcher control over study materials and procedures is of major importance and will be addressed in more detail in the following three chapters. We have also emphasised the need for further empirical validation of Internet-mediated methodologies through comparison with traditional research procedures. Such research will help to answer some of the questions concerning data validity in IMR, though the research to date is generally supportive. Finally we considered the types of data that can be collected over the Internet and the range of procedures that can be implemented. We noted that questionnaires, interviews, observational studies, and experiments are possible. Further, the unique features of the Internet afford new possibilities not available to traditional methods.

Ethical Considerations in Internet-Mediated Research

Conducting primary research on the Internet raises some specific ethical issues. Ensuring that pre-existing ethical standards are properly met can be more difficult, due to the novel features of Internet-mediated procedures. In addition, some new issues arise as a result of the novel features of the Internet environment. The problem (in our opinion) is not so much that adequate ethical procedures cannot be ensured in IMR, as the lack of a set of clear and widely accepted guidelines outlining appropriate and effective procedures. At the time of writing this book these issues are just beginning to be identified and addressed. Here, we are brief in outlining what we see to be the main issues in need of clarification. These are: obtaining informed consent; ensuring security and confidentiality of data; clarifying the private/public distinction; and developing effective debriefing procedures. Later chapters discuss these issues further in relation to specific recommended procedures.

The issue of informed consent arises since it is easier over the Internet for the participant to deceive the researcher. We have already highlighted this problem in relation to data validity. In a traditional setting the researcher obtains informed consent by asking the participant to sign a statement indicating his or her wish to participate. Participants should be 18 years or over to be able to give consent. The problems that arise in relation to IMR are first that it is much easier for participants to lie about their age (researchers have no physical cues to help them judge participants' honesty). It is not yet clear how this problem can be overcome, other than perhaps trying to implement sampling procedures unlikely to attract under 18s. However, this kind of fraudulence may in practice be both rare and easily detected (depending on the nature of the research question and procedure). In IMR, consent may be given by asking the participant to click on a button labelled 'I accept' after having read a paragraph giving some information about the study and procedure. Alternatively, participants may be sent a password via email and asked to enter this in order to take part in the study. Various procedures are imaginable, and selecting the most appropriate will depend on consideration of other features of the study. More research is needed on this (see Smith and Leigh, 1997, for some suggestions).

One recommendation we offer, in helping to ensure that participation is entirely voluntary, is to make it easy for participants to withdraw from the study at any time during the procedure. This may easily be done, for example, by ensuring that a clearly visible 'Withdraw' button is available on the screen throughout the study. At the end of a study a clearly labelled 'Submit data' button should be provided alongside a 'Withdraw' button. These procedures, in addition to explicit pre-study instructions informing participants that participation is entirely voluntary and that they may withdraw at any stage, and asking them to give consent (by any of the methods mentioned), should be enough to meet ethical requirements.

Ensuring confidentiality and security of information provided by the participant is essential. However, the Internet may provide more scope than traditional methods for data being viewed by a third party. For example, it is easier in an email study to send responses to the wrong address by making a minor typing error. Other threats to data security include the scope for hackers to obtain access to files containing confidential information about participants. Chapter 6 discusses this issue in more depth and outlines techniques that can be employed to maximise data security. These procedures are especially important in research dealing with sensitive and personal topics. We consider the recommendations given in Chapter 6 to be adequate in ensuring that ethical requirements for confidentiality of data are met.

Internet-mediated research raises new issues concerning respecting individuals' rights for privacy. The Internet has produced new forms of communication, for example email, interactive chat, newsgroups, published articles, and so on. The issue of the distinction between the private and public domain on the Internet has been raised as an issue (e.g. Jones, 1994) and has yet to be resolved. The crucial question is whether the researcher is ethically justified in using publicly available information as data for a research study. Or, more specifically, in which context is this ethically acceptable or not acceptable? As outlined earlier, Bordia (1996) defends the ethical acceptability of using BITNET discussion group archives as data for naturalistic observation studies. While we expect others to disagree, we propose that using data that have been deliberately and voluntarily made available in the public Internet domain (including on the WWW and in newsgroups) should be accessible to researchers, providing anonymity is ensured. Hacking into individuals' personal files or email accounts, however, is not acceptable. Neither is stumbling over information that was clearly not intended to be made public, and using this. Research is clearly needed on this topic, however, and no doubt as it accumulates our above recommendations will be shown to be far too simplistic.[21]

The final issue highlighted above concerns debriefing. Guidelines typically state that the researcher is ethically responsible for debriefing participants after they have completed the procedure. In traditional approaches this would usually involve a face-to-face verbal explanation of the study, and an invitation for comments or queries. The researcher would also assess whether the participant has suffered any harm as a result of the procedure and take steps to address this if necessary. In IMR this debriefing procedure may be more difficult to enforce. An obvious method would be to send a 'debriefing text' that provides some explanation of the purpose of the study and provides a contact address in case participants require further information. This could be done via a web browser immediately after the participant has submitted his or her data, or by email. However, the point is that it is more difficult for the researcher in this context to monitor whether participants have actually read the debriefing note, and also the extent to which they may have been adversely affected by the procedure. While this is an issue, it is not specific to IMR. Studies that do not involve direct face-to-face interaction between researcher and participant are not so uncommon, and in these cases alternative debriefing arrangements must be made. In our view, ensuring that a debriefing note is sent immediately after the study, which is clearly visible/accessible to participants, and which includes a contact address, is enough. Research is nevertheless needed into the most effective debriefing procedures.

At the time of writing, the above issues are just starting to be acknowledged and addressed, as more careful and thorough consideration of appropriate and effective IMR procedures is emerging. At this stage these issues still need further investigation. However, some guidelines have already been presented: for example, Szabo and Frenkl (1996) list a set of ethical guidelines for IMR. While these are certainly a useful starting point, we do not agree with all of the recommendations made. For example, it is proposed that requesting demographic information from participants should be kept to a minimum, that selection of participants on the basis of ethnicity, religion, income, occupation, or sexual preference should not be attempted, and that studies that address specific ethnic, political, religious, or class issues should not be carried out on the Internet. As noted previously, we stress the importance of gathering demographic information from IMR participants in order to assess sampling biases, evaluate different sampling procedures, and address issues of data validity. Further, we have already argued that a major advantage of IMR is its ability to access special-interest populations and minority groups (ethnic or otherwise). We see no reason for avoiding studies of a political nature on the Internet. Clearly these issues require further discussion to resolve both moral and technical problems. In relation to the latter, solutions are sure to evolve as Internet research procedures and technologies become more sophisticated.

Notes

1   It is worth noting that in addition to posting to newsgroups, the study was advertised by placement on a web site with pointers to on-line research studies.
2   The types of studies that we feel are needed in this area are those that compare Internet- and non-Internet-accessed samples in terms of demographic characteristics, as well as other traits. However, studies that move beyond the use of undergraduate student samples, and Internet samples recruited from psychology-related newsgroups, are needed. The effects of different sampling procedures (discussed later in this chapter) on the types of samples obtained is central to the issue, and also in need of further research.
3   A larger body of literature comparing Internet and traditional samples exists in marketing research-related journals, but emphasis has tended to be on how to increase response rates.
4   A firewall is a set of related programs on a network gateway server that protects the resources of a private network from users of other networks. A firewall controls what access outside users have to data on the private network, as well as what outside resources its own users have access to. The firewall examines each network packet to decide whether to forward it toward its destination (*WhatIs.techtarget.com/*).
5   A proxy server is a server that acts as an intermediary between a workstation user and the Internet. It sits between the client application (for example, web browser) and web server. It can filter requests (for example, to stop users accessing certain web sites).

6 See Mann and Stewart (2000) for further discussion of the groups excluded from having Internet access.

7 This approach of using the WWW to administer stimuli and collect responses, in which the participant uses a web browser to interact with a web server, probably offers the greatest scope in IMR and is discussed at length in Chapter 5.

8 Newsgroups are described in Chapter 2 under 'subject-based discussion groups'.

9 This is at least the case in psychological research. The extent to which other disciplines rely on non-probabilistic samples may vary. However, IMR does not preclude the possibility of obtaining probabilistic samples, as discussed later in this chapter.

10 This issue is discussed by Bradley (1999). Bradley points out the popularity of programs like 'Spam Bait Creator', which automatically creates web pages with bogus email addresses. The intention is that these will be harvested by email address list-sellers and thus reduce the quality of these databases.

11 Dormant email accounts are probably more common than we might think. Many companies allocate email addresses to individuals with the intention of providing training and equipment, yet these accounts can remain unused (Bradley, 1999).

12 This issue of spamming also arises in relation to posting participation calls to newsgroups. As discussed later in this and other chapters, newsgroup moderators can sometimes object to such postings and thus permission should always be sought.

13 An additional problem reported by Dahlen (1998) was that the number of responses far exceeded expectations and this led to server overload that resulted in data loss.

14 However, a more thorough consideration of the problems that may arise and how to forestall and/or recover from these is presented in Chapter 6.

15 Chapter 4 outlines the equipment needed to place a survey or questionnaire on the WWW. Chapter 5 provides details of the programming required.

16 See especially Chapter 6 for discussion on how to guard against hacker mentality.

17 This issue is discussed at length in Chapter 4, and solutions for minimising uncontrolled variation are outlined.

18 See Mann and Stewart (2000, Chap. 6), for further discussion of online interviewing.

19 The distinction between 'direct' and 'indirect' observation has been somewhat unclear, despite the terms being widely used within the social sciences. We find the distinction useful here in order to contrast observations of behaviour in real time and close proximity, which are often possible in traditional observational research, with observations that are possible via computer networks (whereby individuals typically interact by sending typed messages).

20 To put it simply, 'bandwidth' refers to the rate at which data can be transmitted.

21 Another issue that we raised in relation to privacy was whether it is acceptable to send participation requests to individuals' email accounts. We don't see why this differs from sending requests to postal addresses, and advocate its ethical acceptability. Of course, the request should be courteous and informative.

4

Equipment for Internet-Based Research

Computers have been used for research purposes in psychology for many years. When they are used as presentation devices for research studies, for presenting stimuli to, and collecting responses from, the user or participant, they can constitute a highly flexible, interactive medium for presenting a wide range of types of study. Using stand-alone machines, this technique has already proved to be very useful and effective, but it requires the participant's presence in front of the machine in the laboratory, which can be expensive or inconvenient. One use of the Internet is as a delivery system for presentation programs to remote machines, which, in principle at least, greatly increases the potentially available pool of participants and computers for them to use. It also makes it easy to run a group of participants simultaneously on a network of computers, whereas previously they might have been forced to perform the task on a single machine, one at a time.

The pace of development of Internet-related technologies is spectacular by any standard, and any summary will inevitably be obsolete (at least in some details) by the time you read this book. But this is no reason to despair – one of the reasons why the Internet has become so important is that it is regulated by standards that specify minimal requirements for software compliance. So generally, if something works now, it should work in the future, but future developments will extend the range of available techniques and technologies.

Internet, Intranets, and System Diversity

Properly speaking, 'Internet' is the name of a communication protocol (IP = Internet Protocol), which unsurprisingly is central to the communication between your computer and the rest of the world. However, the name has also come to be applied to the global network of computers connected using this protocol; this is perhaps the most common contemporary understanding of the word. It denotes a huge, diverse assemblage of many different types of computers, communicating via a common set of protocols, but ranging from text-only monochrome terminals, at the low end, to powerful PCs, Macintoshes and UNIX workstations, with Windowing systems, high-resolution colour screens, and many configurable interface options, at the high end.

Some computers have multiple users, either at the same time or at different times, and some are used exclusively by a single user. With multi-user systems, many users may be connected simultaneously via a single host, so we must distinguish usernames at the host, since the hostname for each user is the same. An opposite extreme is the single-user PC or workstation, with a unique IP address that can be uniquely traced to the user. Other PCs are used by multiple users in sequence, and of course some users may share usernames in all manner of complicated situations, so it's not advisable to associate hostnames or IP addresses with individual participants without good reason.

A common distinction that will be used in this chapter is between client and server systems: clients typically provide the user interface to a communications system, and servers handle communication and distribution functions, ordinarily on machines that are remote from the user's client machine. The existence of standard protocols allows clients from multiple manufacturers to communicate with servers from other manufacturers, so Internet use is not tied to a particular hardware platform or software manufacturer. For each major Internet technology, such as email or the Web, there are typically several alternative client programs available for any given platform: while some are free, others cost money, and they vary in interface design and the range of functionality available.

Both hardware and software differences are apt to affect the way information is presented to the user. Web content is generally displayed as well as possible on any given hardware, allowing a certain degree of standardisation despite local variations, for example in display resolution or in the range of fonts supported. But interface differences between competing browsers may cause them to present the same pages differently, even on the same hardware. From a research point of view it is problematic that there can be a much greater degree of variation in the hardware and software of the client systems in use than in traditional approaches to computer-based experimentation, since this can introduce experimental error.

This diversity presents problems for certain areas of psychological research, in which the physical properties of the display are of importance, such as psychophysical or speech comprehension research. Researchers in such fields require precise timing of events, control of display properties, and possibly special interface equipment such as button boxes, and none of these things can be guaranteed across the Internet. But it is possible to conduct research over the Internet that is unaffected by this diversity, for example email studies and simple Web-based surveys. This approach is to be recommended if possible, since it can reach the largest possible population.[1] In studies that are likely to be affected by hardware or software variability, it may still be possible to conduct Internet-based research, since it is possible to retrieve some information about client machines. So although we can't control the client machines in advance, we can at least take account of variations afterwards to some extent.

A more recent coinage is 'Intranet', which refers to a local-area Internet network, in a company or educational institution for example, which may or may not be connected to the outside world, but which is private to some extent. Material that is accessible from within an Intranet may not be accessible from outside. This division can be useful if we want to restrict use of a Web-based presentation system to machines in our own department. Many departments in academic institutions have networks of similar machines for students' use and for research purposes, and restricting a program to execute only on these well-known machines can help control against hardware variations. Also, when working with such an Intranet, we are likely to have tighter control of the participant population since we will probably meet our participants, whereas recruiting across the Internet can sometimes result in unexpected and unwelcome surprises.

This type of Intranet-based research is very similar indeed to what psychologists have been doing for years with local-area networks (LANs), namely running a program on each of a network of machines and sending the results to a central server. The difference is the technology: nowadays, the use of an Intranet-based system gives access to a range of attractive new software technologies, and confers a high degree of portability and re-usability on software: Web-based presentation systems have a good chance of running unchanged on other departments' Intranets, whatever hardware they use, as well as being usable directly across the Internet if required.

LANs are also useful for controlled interaction and dialogue studies, and the high bandwidth of a departmental network makes it possible to use live audio and video links with a high degree of fidelity.

Basic Requirements

More or less any reasonably recent computer is capable of connection to the Internet, either directly via a local Ethernet network, or indirectly via the phone system using a modem or ISDN. Most dialup connections use PPP (Point-to-Point Protocol), which effectively emulates a direct connection over the serial modem link, so once connected the machine has essentially the same relation to the Internet as has a directly connected one, with the difference that the bandwidth of the connection is much lower, that is, the rate of data transfer is much lower. This limits the viability of high-bandwidth applications, such as live audio or video links, which might be considered by researchers in dialogue for example.

While many Internet users still connect via 56K modems, more recent 'broadband' (that is, high-bandwidth) access technologies include cable modems, which use cable TV network cables, and Digital Subscriber Line (DSL) systems, which are typically available from telephone companies since they use conventional copper telephone lines. Broadband systems typically offer data transfer rates on the order of hundreds of kilobits per second, although local details will vary.

Software Technologies Useful for Research

Assuming you have a working Internet connection, you have access to a range of technologies that use the Internet.

Telnet and FTP

Telnet and FTP (File Transfer Protocol) once were the basic tools for using the Internet, but both have been broadly eclipsed for most purposes since the development of the World Wide Web, although they remain useful for developers.

FTP is a protocol for transferring files between machines. FTP clients may be command-driven (such as FTP.EXE, distributed with Microsoft Windows, or many common UNIX FTP clients), or they may have graphical interfaces (for example, WS-FTP).

Telnet is a simple program to allow a user to log in to another machine, on which the user will typically have an account. Interaction with the remote machine is through the keyboard only, and the remote machine displays its output in a way that is compatible with a text-only display, so a Telnet connection will work with even the simplest terminals and obsolete PCs. Telnet clients running in more sophisticated windowed environments will usually emulate the once-common DEC VT100 terminals (for example, TELNET.EXE, distributed with MS Windows).

Most contemporary computers have windowing systems and graphical interfaces, and the wide range of superior client technologies for interacting with remote machines make these protocols unattractive for most purposes. If participants are required to download a file, for example, nowadays this facility would normally be provided via the Web, using the browser to download the file using the HTTP protocol, so FTP would not normally be used. Similarly, online interaction with remote machines would normally be provided via a browser or other specialist client system, so Telnet is not likely to be employed. However, it is possible that some users will only have World Wide Web access via

Lynx, the text-only Web browser, running under VT100 emulation over a Telnet connection. Vision-impaired users who use text-to-speech or other specialist systems may also be effectively restricted to web pages which can be displayed this way. Web developers who want to be accessible to the widest possible population should bear such limitations in mind, and test their pages for accessibility using text-only browsers.

Email and USENET News

Email requires an email client (for example, Eudora, Pegasus, Pine on UNIX, Netscape Mail, Microsoft Outlook or Outlook Express) and an email account. Email is perhaps the most straightforward and easy Internet technology to use, requiring little specialist or programming knowledge once it has been configured. Hewson and Vogel (1994) used email to administer surveys to a large population recruited through advertisements placed on USENET newsgroups. Such a use of email differs little in principle from the traditional methods for administering surveys, by post or by telephone. Since responses are in plain text, there is limited scope for automating data analysis when using such a method.

Participant recruitment by USENET news requires a news client (for example, Netscape Communicator on all platforms, Forte Agent or Free Agent on MS Windows, Outlook or Outlook Express on Windows) and the address of a news server.

Hewson and Vogel used USENET newsgroups for calls to participate in surveys, and this technique can reach a very large population of potential participants. Although the lists of available newsgroups offered by different servers are likely to differ in places, there are newsgroups that cater to almost any lifestyle choice, so it is possible to find specialist populations of many different kinds. But the effectiveness of the method depends on whether your chosen newsgroup really does have a large, active population of subscribers; merely because you can find *rec.pets. aardvark* in a list of available groups, you should not assume that all, or even any, true aardvark enthusiasts will subscribe to it. Even groups that for a time support a genuine community of interested users are apt to be undermined by large volumes of spam (crossposted advertisements and general junk) or flame wars (escalating battles in which some subscribers trade abuse), which can result in the effective death of newsgroups. To combat this type of problem, some newsgroups are moderated by certain individuals who ensure that postings are on-topic, so in such cases you may need to negotiate with such a person to get your message posted.

Since news distribution is patchy, you may not reach as wide an audience as you might expect. It takes time, possibly several days, before a message is likely to have a chance of reaching all news servers in the world, since the volume of news in circulation is huge, and servers have limited transfer and storage capacity. Depending on the available storage space and the amount of incoming material, messages may expire (be deleted) relatively quickly on some servers, making those messages effectively invisible to users of those servers. The USENET protocol offers a number of options, which can be set via message header lines, by which you can influence these factors. The default distribution is 'world', which gives the message a chance to be distributed to all news servers in the world. You can restrict distribution to your own, local news server by specifying

Distribution: local

Alternatively, to restrict distribution to a specific country or top-level domain, specify the appropriate country code or domain, without the leading dot (for example, 'uk', 'ie', 'edu' or 'com') in place of 'local'.

Similarly you can set expiry dates to ensure that your message will expire by a certain time (unfortunately, however, you cannot ensure that the message will survive for as long as you specify). To do this, use an 'Expires:' header with the intended date and time, like so:

Expires: Fri, 07 Apr 2000 08:40:52 +0000

Newsgroup etiquette and posting restrictions are discussed further in Chapter 6.

Multimedia

Streaming audio and video protocols allow audio and video clips, or even live channels, to be broadcast across the Internet and played on client machines using client software such as RealNetworks' RealPlayer. It would thus be possible to use these technologies to present extended audio or video materials as stimuli, perhaps as part of a more complex system. Unfortunately at the time of writing, when Internet access is primarily by dialup modems, the limited bandwidth available ensures that sound fidelity is poor, and video is restricted to jerky, low-resolution onscreen images little bigger than a postage stamp.

An alternative to delivering audio materials in real time is to distribute sound files, for download and replay on the client machine, in the MP3 format. This uses data compression to allow download of audio files with reasonable fidelity in reasonable time, although the file size is still considerable. Video can be done this way too, with even greater bandwidth restrictions. There are other specialised technologies for delivering music over the Net, which might be useful in some situations.

Of course, using audio stimulus materials will only work if client machines all have properly configured audio facilities, and suitable installed software, such as RealPlayer or an MP3 player, and this cannot be ensured generally. Also, these technologies in themselves offer no useful means for interaction by participants, and without interaction there is no research study, so they would need to be augmented with other technologies to constitute a complete system. This restricts their usefulness for delivering materials over the Internet, given that client machines would have to be properly prepared before running the task, but such technologies may still be useful in a more controlled environment with greater bandwidth, such as a departmental local-area network.

Interactive Chat

A popular application of the Internet is interactive chat, which allows groups of users to participate in real-time online text-based discussion. There are several different technologies, such as Internet Relay Chat (IRC) and ICQ ('I seek you'), which achieve this end in different ways. The basic mode of operation of IRC, for example, is the group chat, although pairs or groups of users can go into privacy if required. ICQ, by contrast, typically sets up a single conversation between two users, although others can join in.

IRC is sometimes compared to Citizens' Band radio, since it allows individuals to participate in public discussions in real time. It makes use of channels, whose names begin with '#' (such as '#chat'), which provide forums for group discussions, and separate them by topic, rather like USENET newsgroups. Channels are routed through one or more servers, and can be created or moderated by a person known as an operator (or 'op'), who sets the topic for discussion. Users who meet in a public channel can easily create private channels for one-to-one or small group discussions. Typical clients for IRC are mIRC, Pirch or Virc for Windows, and Homer or Ircle for the Macintosh.

ICQ aims to provide primarily private, direct channels for communication between two or more users. It addresses a common problem, that it is difficult to open a direct channel between two users when the initiator of the conversation does not know whether the other person is online at any given time, and furthermore does not know the IP address of his or her computer when he or she is online, since this tends to change every time due to dynamic IP addressing (as discussed below). The ICQ client solves this problem by remaining resident in users' computers, and monitoring their dialup connections; when they go online, it tells the ICQ server that they are online, and what their current IP address is, allowing other users to know whether they are available for a chat at that time. The ICQ client displays a list of the user's friends or associates, identified by nicknames, as well as their current online availability, and provides a chat interface to make the whole process of setting up a conversation transparent. As well as text-based chat, ICQ can also be used to set up audio connections for voice interaction.

Clients for each type of chat system allow logging of conversations, which is essential for data-gathering purposes. To monitor an ICQ session, a researcher can sit in as a silent participant in a conversation, and log the conversation to disk; this can be played back in real time or at a variety of speeds, since the log includes event times for individual keystrokes. While this type of facility is welcome, the timings are inevitably subject to network delays, and it seems that the ICQ playback program only updates its displayed time every 10 seconds, so accuracy in timing is not to be expected. To monitor IRC sessions, it may be preferable to set up and moderate a special channel, and use this as the location for the conversation. Researchers should remember that it is ethical good practice to inform participants that they are being monitored.

Novices usually find chat systems difficult to use at first, so it would be advisable to give participants training before the study itself; altern-atively, you may prefer to recruit experienced users, using appropriate public IRC channels to advertise the study.

Using the World Wide Web for Research

The Web is now the most important delivery system for primary research materials on the Internet. Web browsers such as Lynx, Mosaic, Opera, Netscape Navigator, and Microsoft Internet Explorer can be used to present stimuli and collect responses, sending the data back to the researcher automatically. The range of functionality supported by web browsers is highly diverse: browsers can display text, graphics, anima-tions and even more sophisticated embedded interactive programs, called 'applets', giving a large palette from which to construct task-presentation systems.

Browsers on client machines interact with remote machines known as web servers, which provide the documents to the client machines, and to which client machines return data. As well as serving up static HTML documents, servers can run programs that generate HTML output on the fly, and these are known as server-side scripts.

HyperText Mark-up Language (HTML)

HTML (HyperText Mark-up Language) is the basis of the World Wide Web: web pages are made out of it. Many researchers will have at least a little experience with HTML by now, since most academic departments encourage the maintenance of personal homepages. For such purposes, an HTML editor such as HoTMetaL or Claris Homepage, or the built-in editors in Netscape Communicator or Microsoft Internet Explorer, may be quite adequate. However, it is likely that for primary research purposes, more knowledge of raw HTML, and of a number of other technologies such as client-side and server-side scripting, will be helpful. This sounds daunting, but much can be learned by simply creating HTML documents in an HTML editor, then looking at the results in a text editor, and modifying them by hand – it is really not very difficult (see also Chapter 5).

HTML is designed primarily with a view to flexibility – the raw document might not specify formatting or specific typeface information, since the intention is to make the document capable of being displayed on as many different hardware platforms as possible. This makes it difficult precisely to control the appearance of stimulus materials. If a particular browser cannot understand a particular HTML tag, it will simply ignore it, and, less drastically, different browsers, or differently configured instances of the same browser, may display text in different fonts with different layouts.

The received wisdom in the world of HTML programming is that developers should try to create code that will work, somehow, on as many different types of browser as possible, so writing HTML that can only be displayed properly by, say, Internet Explorer 4 is generally frowned upon. This restriction prioritises accessibility, and should not be flouted lightly. However, for the purposes of experimental procedures, restricting access to a particular browser type may sometimes be acceptable, since specific knowledge of the client browser's capabilities can help control display variation, or it might be the case that only a particular browser supports the functionality we need.

Most modern web browsers support at least HTML 3.2 or HTML 4.0, but most HTML versions permit a range of data types, particularly text and static inline graphics, to be presented in a set of linked pages, along with a range of interactive devices. Using forms, data can be sent from the client browser to the server (using a server-side CGI script to handle the data, see server-side scripting section below), or via email to a mailbox, permitting feedback of results to researchers. Standard form elements are buttons, text input boxes, checkboxes, and radio buttons – checkboxes operate independently whereas radio buttons are linked together, permitting a single selection from a range of options, so properly formatted they can also be used as discrete-interval rating scales. Figure 4.1 shows examples of these uses of different types of form elements in an obviously non-existent survey (see Chapter 5 for details on constructing a survey page like this).

Simple, HTML-only web pages with forms can be used as convenient, user-friendly substitutes for email surveys. Ordinary HTML allows presentations with several pages, accessible in a fixed order or at the

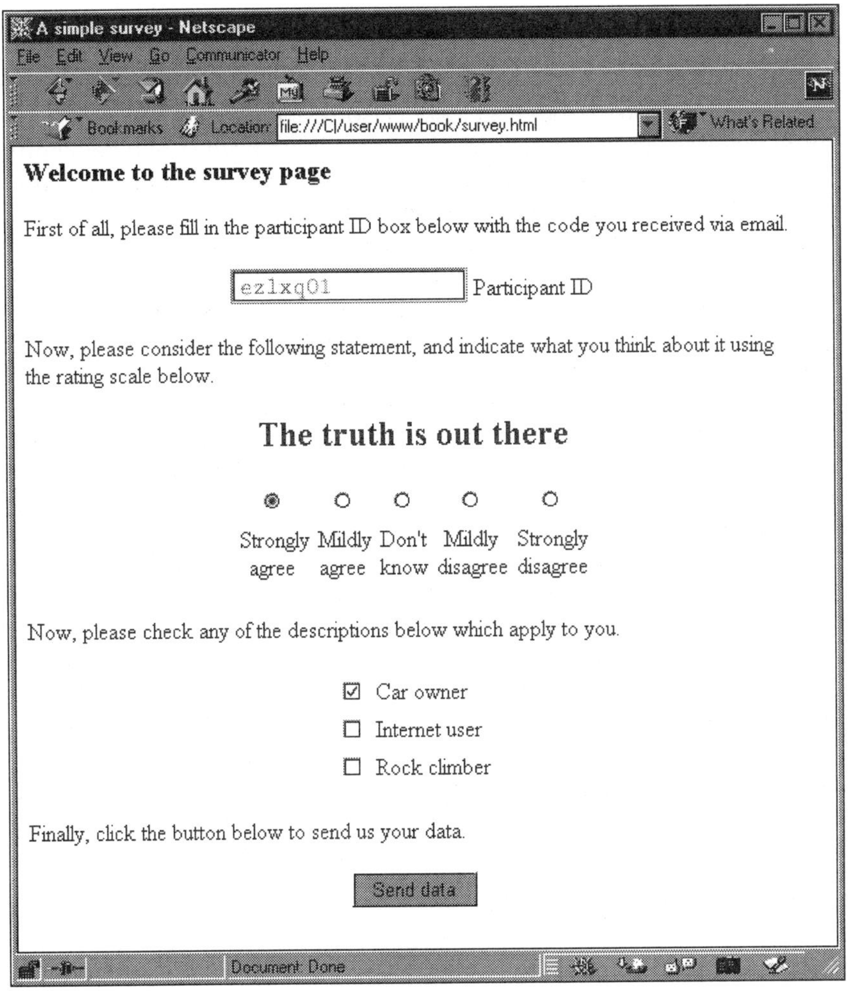

Figure 4.1   *A simple survey, using HTML forms*

participant's discretion, depending on how the pages are interlinked. Controlled randomisation of presentation order is not possible with plain HTML, but using server-side or client-side scripts does allow such randomisation (see below, Chapter 5).

Web Servers

To make your HTML documents available over the Web, they must be placed on a web server. This is a computer, generally with a permanent network connection, which is running web server software. The software responds to HTTP requests for documents, which it then sends to the machine that made the request, or client. Common web server programs are Apache on UNIX machines, and Microsoft's Internet Information Server on Windows 2000. (Microsoft also distributes a simpler version called Personal Information Server.)

Depending on your requirements, it may not be necessary to know much about the server, other than where to put your documents; this is especially the case if you don't want the reader of your documents to send you any data (which is unlikely in a research situation), or if the data will be sent by email. Normally, though, a study will require at least a small amount of server-side scripting to permit data return.

In most cases it will not be necessary to operate your own server, since most academic departments have one nowadays, and you can discuss your requirements with your local webmaster; this also applies if you need to host your pages in the private domain. It is worth knowing, though, that the server can be used to gather useful data about your participants. It is fairly easy to log client machines' names or addresses, and even individual usernames when appropriate. It is also possible to log the location of the page where the user encountered the link by which they arrived at your own page; this is useful if the study has been advertised in several locations, and the researcher wants to monitor sampling, as discussed in Chapter 3 (and see Chapter 5 for more details). If you operate the server itself, then you will have access to all the log files; however, even if you just use server-side scripts, you can still gather such information for your own use, provided the required functionality is enabled by your webmaster.

Server-Side Scripting

Server-side scripting uses special-purpose programs that execute on the server, to give the server more power and flexibility in determining what is sent to the client and when. It also permits the on-line parsing of form submissions to collect and save data from the client. This is a powerful technique, and is universally supported by web browsers using the Common Gateway Interface (CGI), but it is considerably less straight-forward than simple HTML, because it requires programming expertise (using Perl, C, or some other language supported by the server), and because it entails construction of a complex system with multiple inter-acting elements. Also, given the likelihood of considerable network delays, over-use of server-side scripting can result in slow, unreliable performance.

Although most researchers using HTML forms will require at least a small amount of server-side scripting, to handle submitted data if nothing else, this much can be achieved relatively easily. On UNIX machines, a small shell script like that described in Chapter 5 may be sufficient if all we require is to save the raw data for all participants to a single file, or send the data via email to a suitable address.

This minimal technique should work adequately for some researchers, but more generally, server scripts can be written in just about any language you like, provided they can handle form data as input, and write HTML as output. The raw input will be encoded (see Chapter 5 for examples), but many languages now include web interfaces that transparently decode the input, allowing it to be easily manipulated and saved in a more accessible format. Such web interfaces often provide facilities to assist in the generation of HTML output, and forms too. With a bit of effort, it is feasible to create sophisticated and flexible systems that can, for example, assign participants to multiple groups in a balanced way, interact in complex ways with the client, collate data, tabulate results, and perform statistics.

Some web servers permit server-side scripting in Java, JavaScript, VBScript, or other languages, bypassing the standard CGI. Such techniques can improve server performance, which is important if you anticipate high volumes of server traffic, and of course it can be convenient to use a language that is already familiar.

Bypassing server-side scripting

An even easier method to send data, from an HTML form on the client back to the researcher, uses the browser's built-in email functions.[2] Although this is simple to program, since it requires no server-side scripting, it assumes that the client browser has been properly configured to send email. This cannot be ensured across the Internet, since some users may habitually use another mail client, so in general it's probably worthwhile to use at least something like the minimal server script described in Chapter 5.

Client-Side Scripting

JavaScript

For some purposes server-side scripts are indispensable (for example, when it is unfeasible or undesirable to send all the data involved in the study to the client, as in the case of applications involving large databases), but recently, powerful client-side scripting languages have become available, such as Netscape's JavaScript (Netscape 2.0, IE 3.0, and subsequent versions of both browsers), which can reduce or eliminate the need for server-side scripts. Since JavaScript is quite a powerful scripting language, it is capable of handling arbitrarily complex tasks, especially those involving text or simple inline graphics, so the need for interaction with complex server-side scripts, and the consequent amount of network traffic, can be greatly reduced.

JavaScript is not Java (see below); it is a simple object-oriented language that can be used to generate HTML pages on the fly, on the client machine, instead of downloading simple static files from the server as usual. JavaScript writes HTML to the web browser's display, which displays the results as if it had downloaded an HTML file, so anything that is possible with standard HTML is also possible with JavaScript. JavaScript programs can also read form elements in the display, providing it with a mechanism to respond to user input (see Chapter 5). In Microsoft's Internet Explorer (versions 3.0 and above), a similar language called JScript is broadly compatible with JavaScript, so with care you can write portable code that will work on both browsers (see below).

Therefore, for example, a task presentation program written in JavaScript can generate randomised blocks of trials, then on each trial it can present a stimulus page containing a form, and collect the data by reading the contents of the form, without the need to submit the form in the conventional sense; it is only at the end of the task that the program needs to send the data. This means that tasks can be performed offline, an important consideration if participants have dialup Internet access: a participant can download the program, hang up the modem, and perform the task offline, only going online again at the end of the session in order to upload the data.

It is possible to open multiple browser windows using JavaScript, and read from and write to them separately. Moreover, these windows can be configured in various ways, for example by setting a given window's size onscreen, and by specifying whether it permits standard browsing functions. This makes it possible to provide an onscreen instruction sheet at the same time as the task in a separate window, if required, or alternatively to force the task window to fill the screen once created.

JavaScript functions can be invoked by mouse events, such as clicking a button or hyperlink, or by other events associated with HTML, such as the loading or unloading of a page, or the submission of a form. Since JavaScript also has time functions, timings are possible via this mechanism, so, for example, the program can present a stimulus, including response buttons, then start the timer, allowing the function that is attached to a response button to record the response time when it is eventually invoked by the participant's mouse-click (see Chapter 5).

However, care is needed to avoid the possibility of timing errors due to network delays, if the display entails downloading extra data, such as graphic files, or even errors due to the speed of the client machine, since displaying a page may take an appreciable interval on slower machines. Also, it is important to note that timings are at the mercy of the client machine's clock, and sometimes multitasking operating systems can cause small timing errors, so do not expect high precision, but timings in the region of modest fractions of a second should be perfectly feasible. Researchers who demand accuracy over shorter time scales (say with millisecond accuracy) will often demand a much higher degree of control of the situation than will ordinarily be possible in the Internet scenario, but for some purposes, provided the client machines are well known, as in an Intranet, and sufficiently powerful, then with careful calibration this degree of accuracy may be possible. It is up to the researcher to verify that the client machines conform to the requirements of the study.

Example: A reasoning experiment in JavaScript. An example of an experimental presentation program, which presents 144 temporal reasoning problems in random order, collects conclusions, and saves them for a single, final data submission, is shown in Figure 4.2. At the left of the screen there is an initial instruction page, written in conventional HTML, which presents instructions for the task. The link at the bottom of the page starts the JavaScript presentation program in a separate window (bottom right), and this makes use of frames to separate a control region from the main problem presentation and response region. The participant is expected to type a conclusion into the text input box, and in this case the JavaScript program syntax-checks the conclusion and prompts

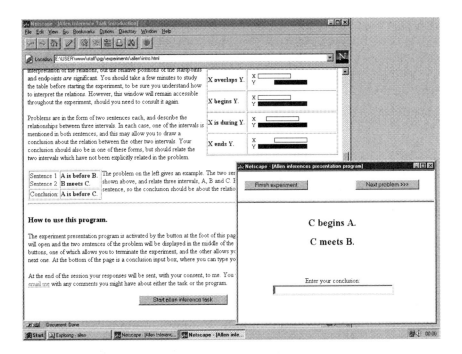

Figure 4.2   *The Allen Inferences experiment*

the participant to try again in the event of a syntax error. Since the script is event-driven, times of events (for example, checking a box or clicking a button) could easily be recorded.

Although this is a fairly simple example of the use of JavaScript, much more sophisticated designs are possible using Dynamic HTML (see below).

VBScript and JScript

Microsoft's Internet Explorer browser supports VBScript, a variant of Visual Basic, as an alternative to JavaScript, which it also supports under the name of JScript. On Internet Explorer, VBScript and JScript are just syntactic alternatives, with the same functionality, but JScript and JavaScript differ in some areas of functionality, despite being broadly compatible.

Some users with Basic programming experience may find VBScript more palatable than JavaScript/JScript, which appeals more to programmers familiar with C or C++, but since VBScript only works with Internet Explorer which is not available on all platforms, it's probably preferable to use JavaScript/JScript for the sake of full cross-platform and cross-browser portability, and test for compatibility with as many configurations as possible.

Recently, VBScript has given rise to widespread security worries owing to its ability to facilitate the spread of email worms and viruses, so many users may be disposed to disable it, and it may be unwise to assume its availability even on Windows machines.

Dynamic HTML

The original HTML specification was restricted in many ways, allowing only static, unchanging content with limited interactivity through the use of forms. While it was possible to display non-interactive animated graphics using the GIF89 standard, and even to create dynamically updated displays by use of frames coupled with JavaScript scripting, such expedients were quite limited in flexibility and required careful design.

However, recent browsers (Netscape 4, IE 4) support Dynamic HTML (DHTML), which allows a much greater degree of interactivity between the user/participant and the content of a web page. Much of the power of DHTML derives from the concept of a layer, a separately encapsulated block of HTML content that can be positioned absolutely on the page using co-ordinates, and with which JavaScript can interact. For example, a layer can be made visible or invisible in response to a mouse-click, or moved or resized dynamically by dragging the mouse pointer. This can be very useful for creating different types of interface device, such as buttons that display text when clicked (made by superimposing two layers, one on top of the other – when the topmost is clicked, it becomes invisible, revealing the one beneath). Such a device could be useful to create computer-based versions of paradigms in which cards are turned over, such as Wason's Four-Card problem (Wason and Johnson-Laird, 1972). Another useful trick is to create invisible layers at the beginning of the trial, which are revealed selectively to give feedback in response to user interaction.

Unfortunately, contemporary browsers use different standards for DHTML, so if you want your client system to work with both Netscape and Internet Explorer, you will have to write separate JavaScript and JScript sections to deal with both possibilities. And while Netscape supports a special <LAYER> tag to define layers, Internet Explorer does not. So, for maximum portability, to define a layer that will work in both types of browser, it is necessary to treat it as an absolutely positioned block of HTML content in Cascading Style Sheet (CSS) syntax, which is mostly portable between the browsers. Then you will need to write separate JavaScript and JScript handlers to deal with the remaining differences between them.

Example: A button-based interface using DHTML. Figure 4.3 shows an example of a client that uses JavaScript and DHTML to implement a

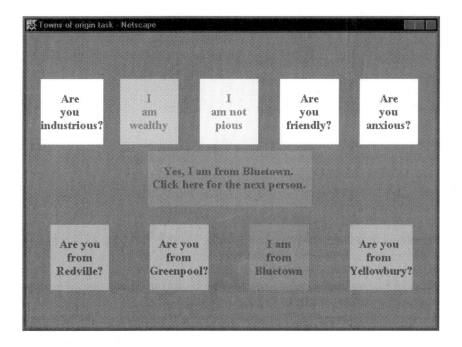

Figure 4.3 *A client that uses JavaScript and DHTML*

button-based interface for a decision-making task. Across a series of trials, participants learn to determine a town of origin of an imaginary person from a set of properties, which they may query by clicking on the buttons on the top row. When clicked, the buttons each reveal whether the imaginary person does or does not have the property; actually they are each composed of two layers, one above the other, and when the link on the top layer is clicked, it is made invisible, revealing the layer beneath. Participants select what they think is the town of origin by clicking on one of the buttons in the bottom row, which work the same way, but which also reveal the box in the centre when clicked. By using event capture, any click within a button's boundary can be routed to the textual links on its top layer, and of course all click events can be timed and logged if desired.

Java   Yet more sophisticated interactive designs are possible using Java (developed by Sun Microsystems Inc.), which is now widely available. There are various Java-enabled browsers, such as Netscape Navigator 2.0 and above, Sun's own HotJava, Opera, and Microsoft Internet Explorer.

Java is an object-oriented programming language that permits animated graphics as well as all the rest of the features of a full programming language, but it does require a powerful client machine (at least a good Pentium or equivalent with more than 16Mb of memory and a 32-bit operating system). Java development requires rather more investment of effort than does development using one of the scripting languages, but it offers the researcher much greater power to produce sophisticated task presentation systems with interactive graphics.

Java applets (small applications or programs, embedded in HTML pages) are delivered across the Web as required, and (in theory at least) function identically on all platforms. While Sun has had problems ensuring that all licensees implemented Java entirely according to its reference specification, better compliance can be expected in the future. Much effort has been expended to ensure that Java programs cannot compromise the security of the client machine, for example by crashing, or by writing to local disk drives. It is therefore a good choice of platform on which to develop Web-based research studies that demand sophisticated graphics or interface options.

However, Java has one disadvantage that has limited its usefulness up to now: Java programs tend to be quite large, and so they are slow to download across the dialup modem links with which most users currently access the Net. This can be mitigated, to some extent, by writing small, reusable applets that can be stored in browser caches. This approach works well if you use an applet that can be embedded in several different web pages. An increasing range of small, special-purpose Java applets is becoming available; these can be embedded in web pages to provide special interface devices, such as sliders or other interactive graphical widgets, in addition to the limited range offered by HTML forms. The idea is to use applets as components of more complex page designs involving HTML and JavaScript, and some useful applets are available 'off the shelf' for use without any special Java programming knowledge. You can find a variety of applets online via the TUCOWS site (see below).

It is worth mentioning that current HTML and DHTML standards do not support vector (line) graphics, which can be very useful for some types of study. Imagine, for example, an experiment on perceptual illusions: while these could be presented as static bitmap images (for example, JPG or GIF files) in some paradigms, the ability to drag line drawings to the 'correct' perceptual size would obviously increase the range of possible experimental manipulations. If such facilities are required, some good lightweight drawing applets are available online free of charge, such as JAIMEAS (available from TUCOWS) which supports vector graphics, interactive animation using combinations of bitmaps and line graphics, and interactivity with JavaScript.

Recently a number of integrated design and presentation systems for experiments and surveys have become available, allowing researchers the ability to design and present tasks with minimal programming; these are discussed in more detail in Chapter 5.

ActiveX   ActiveX is a name for a proprietary Microsoft technology (available only in Internet Explorer) by means of which applets can be embedded in web pages, extending the range of graphical and interface options, so in some respects it is similar to Java. However, there are two main differences: first, ActiveX applets are not portable across different hardware platforms, so they will only work on Intel machines running Windows; and, second, they are not secure in the way that Java applets are. ActiveX applets, once started, can in principle do anything, reading or writing the hard disk, spreading viruses or mis-behaving in many possible ways. As a software author, you may be quite confident that your applet won't compromise the user's security, but users may be unwilling to trust a technology that lacks built-in safeguards.

While ActiveX applets will run on most machines, simply because most machines are Intel-based, and run Windows and Internet Explorer, their inability to work on all platforms still limits their applicability. Java does not suffer from these problems, so many developers will prefer it.

Tracking Participants

As we have emphasised throughout this book, it is difficult to ensure that participants in online studies are who they say they are. One way to approach the question of individual identity, which is commonly employed in the online world, is to associate individual people with individual computers or individual user accounts on computers. This section argues against this approach.

Individual computers are often identifiable by means of their IP address, which is a group of four positive integers, each in the range 0–255, separated by dots. While IP addresses are fundamental to Internet addressing, they are not easy for humans to process, so a parallel system of textual host names exists. Thus for example, *holyrood.ed.ac.uk* is the textual version of 129.215.16.14. Textual host names are automatically translated to IP addresses when required, by Domain Name Servers (DNSs).

IP addresses provide unique identifiers for machines that are permanently connected to the Net, such as machines on Ethernet networks. However, many machines are connected to the Internet only by dialup links across telephone lines, and usually in such cases IP addresses are assigned dynamically from a pool of addresses owned by the Internet Service Provider (local-area networks configured to use DHCP also do this). Thus a client machine's IP address will change every time it connects to the ISP or network, and so an IP address cannot be reliably associated with an individual machine across multiple sessions.

To overcome this indeterminacy in addressing, the HyperText Transfer Protocol provides 'cookies': a mechanism to allow servers to track client machines across multiple sessions, irrespective of their IP addresses. A cookie is a way for the server to store a small amount of information on the client machine when the client interacts with it, and which the client sends back to it in subsequent transactions, perhaps after some considerable time. Thus the server knows that this client has accessed its site before, and can recover any additional information that has been stored in the cookie from earlier sessions.

From a technical point of view, it is possible to set cookies from either the server or the client by using special functions built in to the standard scripting languages. Cookies are stored internally as character strings, typically a few tens of characters in length. While this data storage capacity is not large, it is quite feasible to set, say, a username and a few parameter values to be accessed at a later date.

On the face of it, then, cookies might appear to be useful tools for tracking participants across multiple sessions. However, there are difficulties with the use of cookies, owing to widespread concerns about security, which limit their usefulness in practice. Some users will deliberately configure their browsers to reject all cookies, out of fear that their privacy could be compromised, so their systems will not work properly with program code that relies on saving cookies.

More importantly, though, researchers should be reminded that tracking computers, whether with cookies or with IP addresses, is not equivalent to tracking participants. The same machine may be used by many users, for example it could be a machine in a public terminal room or cybercafé, or it could be a family PC with several different users. Even individual user accounts on a single machine cannot be assumed to have a single user, so while each user account has a separate cookie store, you still cannot be sure that it is the same person who is at the keyboard every time.

To emphasise the point, cookies are not recommended as a sole means for tracking real human participants in real research situations. It is better to issue consenting participants with a user ID, and to request that they keep it secret, and that they enter it on each occasion of use – that way they can use different machines on each occasion if necessary, and they will not be mistaken for other participants, who can use their own ID codes on the same machine if necessary. Another benefit of this approach is that it can be used to control access to materials – the user ID can act as a password to access the system, allowing the system to deny access to anyone other than the approved participant, if this is desired.

Conclusions and Caveats

This chapter has discussed some of the most widespread Internet technologies suitable for primary research. Doubtless many readers can imagine other approaches that have not been mentioned here, using different types of software and protocols. While such approaches may be perfectly feasible (and we do not wish to discourage creative use of technology), it is always worth considering whether the target population has access to the software required. People can only participate in a study if they have the appropriate software installed and configured, so an effective approach is to use systems that are already highly widespread and widely used (say, email or web browsers). If participants are required to install special software and learn new systems, many will be discouraged from participating, either because of the time and difficulty involved, the download costs (several megabytes for most contemporary client packages), or even because they do not trust unknown software on their systems. Thus the use of more exotic technologies will inevitably reduce the size of the accessible population.

Even in more controlled situations, such as departmental Intranets, participants' levels of knowledge and experience can cause difficulties. In studies using web browser technology and undergraduate student samples, some participants have little idea how to use a web browser, even when considerable efforts have been expended to make the interface as simple and transparent as possible. Sometimes they seem to worry that they should not trust the instructions the program is giving them, as if they assume that the software contains an error, or that the instructions on the screen are not intended for them. For example, at the end of one study, the browser window displayed a message saying 'The experiment is over. You may now close this window', which prompted several people to check with the researcher whether this was true? Such difficulties are generally easy to resolve when the researcher is present, but could cause substantial disruption when help is not immediately available, such as when the materials are delivered across the Internet.

In the Intranet case, it is even dangerous to assume basic familiarity with computers, or with the particular platform you are using – a friend has confessed that when he recently upgraded to a Windows machine, after years using only MSDOS, he had no idea how to use a mouse, and needed detailed instructions; we have also encountered some undergraduates with the same difficulty. Participants will usually be uncomfortable when using technologies of which they know little, and such factors can influence the results, for example by depressing performance levels on the computer-based task relative to a task using more conventional technologies such as paper.

Ease of use is always an important consideration when writing software, but especially so when the user is likely to encounter it only once. While in the general case, a user can overcome a difficult interface if necessary by repeated exposure, in the research case the interface needs to be transparent and to work immediately, first time, with minimal effort on the user's part. Interface problems can cause the sample to be skewed, when some classes of users are unable to complete the study for technical reasons, or, worse, they may return meaningless data that bias the results.

Where to Find Software and Documentation

There are many good software archives on the Web, but the software packages discussed in this chapter, and many more, can be found via the excellent TUCOWS site, at *www.tucows.com/*. This site lists software packages, provides reviews and information about online availability and cost, and links to homepages for individual packages.

There is extensive technical documentation on HTML, Java, JavaScript, and other Netscape-supported technologies at *developer.netscape.com/*.

Information on development for Microsoft products such as Internet Explorer can be found at *msdn.microsoft.com/*.

Notes

1 However, as noted in Chapter 3, not all research aims to obtain large, diverse samples. Nevertheless, access to a large population may help in obtaining small numbers of 'rare case' participants and so is also useful in cases when wide generalisability is not the aim.

2 Hint: use a 'mailto:email@address' ACTION with the POST submit method.

5

How to Design and Implement an Internet Survey

In Chapter 3 it was noted that the survey methodology has been identified as the most widely used technique in social research. It is certainly true, at the time of writing, that surveys and questionnaires are the most widely implemented Web-based research methodology. Thus it seems appropriate to devote a chapter to discussing design issues and software procedures for implementing survey-based research on the Internet. Surveys can range from structured questionnaires to unstructured interviews. The typical Web survey involves a structured questionnaire. A general discussion of the scope for implementing questionnaires and interviews in IMR was given in Chapter 3. Here we develop that discussion further by providing enough detail to get a Web survey up and running. In the sections that follow we cover survey design issues and software procedures, giving examples of programming code and procedures as necessary. The focus here is upon structured survey approaches, since these are widely used across many disciplines within the social and behavioural sciences, and because they tend to involve more complex implementation procedures in an IMR context than do unstructured approaches. The techniques we discuss, however, are suitable for both structured and unstructured approaches. A more detailed discussion of the issues particular to carrying out unstructured interviews using the Internet can be found in Mann and Stewart (2000).

Design Issues

There is a mass of information on factors involved in survey methodology in the context of traditional approaches (for example, Kalton and Shuman, 1982; Kanuk and Berenson, 1975; Sudman, 1980). At this stage in the development of Web-based surveys, there is very little published research on the factors that will influence design decisions, such as factors affecting response rate, response bias, non-response bias, sincerity of responses, completion of responses, length of responses, and so on.[1] We propose here not to review the immense body of literature on traditional survey research, but rather to highlight some aspects of survey design that have been outlined as particularly important, and which we believe may well be relevant in an IMR context also. Our main focus is to outline some detailed procedures that are useful in producing a Web-based survey, taking into account design issues based on prior findings and our own experience and insights. Clearly, there is a need for more research into the factors that will impact upon Internet-based survey research procedures. The advice we offer here is a starting point, which we hope will help to instigate further research in this area within the social and behavioural sciences.

Postal Surveys

A vast body of research into traditional postal survey methodology exists. During the fifties, sixties, and seventies a large number of studies focused on identifying factors that can affect survey responses. This research has addressed a range of issues, focusing particularly on how factors such as survey presentation format, question length and type, levels of anonymity, personalisation, incentives, and sponsorship influence response rates, response bias, non-response bias, and response error. A review of the literature on response rates and response and non-response bias in postal mail surveys is presented by Kanuk and Berenson (1975). They highlight several factors that the literature suggests are influential in affecting survey response. First they report that follow-ups or reminders are almost universally shown to be successful in increasing response rates, and that preliminary notification is also effective in increasing response rates. Affiliation with an official or respected organisation (such as a university), inclusion of a return envelope, postage by special delivery, and advance money incentives have also been shown to help increase response rates in mail surveys (Kanuk and Berenson, 1975). Factors that received little support in terms of increasing response rates were questionnaire length, personalisation, promise of anonymity, and size, colour, and reproduction of questionnaires. In relation to response bias, studies have focused on demographic, socioeconomic, and personality variables; Kanuk and Berenson report that the only widespread finding is that respondents tend to be better educated than non-respondents.[2]

Sheehan and McMillan (1999) have more recently reviewed some findings in relation to postal mail surveys, confirming that response rates can be increased by preliminary notification (Fox et al., 1988), as can response speed (Murphy et al., 1991; Taylor and Lynn, 1998). Incentives were also identified as increasing response rates (Fox et al., 1988; Goyder, 1982). However, Sheehan and McMillan cite evidence that shorter questionnaire length can increase response rates (Yammarino et al., 1991), whereas Kanuk and Berenson (1975) found evidence for this lacking. Fox et al. (1998) and Goyder (1982) both found affiliation with a university, results in higher response rates than does affiliation with a corporation. Sheehan and McMillan also identified 'issue salience' as something that contributes in determining response rates – that is, the more engaging, interesting, and relevant respondents find the research topic, the more likely they will be to respond (Heberlein and Baumgartner, 1978; Martin, 1994).

In sum the evidence indicates that follow-ups, preliminary notifications, and affiliation with a respected organisation are factors that have been clearly shown to increase response rates. These factors are easy to incorporate into an IMR survey, depending on the particular approach adopted. These factors will be discussed in relation to different approaches below. It cannot be presumed that these factors will necessarily have the same impact in an Internet context, and further research is needed. Personalisation and questionnaire length have some support for influencing survey responses, and again are factors that we feel should be considered in Internet survey research. As discussed below, there is some evidence that in Internet surveys questionnaire length is an issue.

Internet Surveys

While there is a mass of online surveys on the World Wide Web,[3] there is still little published research on the factors that influence participants' responses in Internet-administered surveys. As noted above, most empirical investigations of Internet survey methodology to date have appeared in market research journals (such as *The International Journal of Market Research* and *Public Opinion Quarterly*) and focus on response rates in Internet (particularly email) surveys, especially how these compare with postal mail response rates and which features can enhance response rates. Market researchers have clearly recognised the potential of the Internet to provide a tool that could lead to acquisition of very large sample sizes at very low cost. Some authors have predicted that Internet survey methodology will provide the basis for market research in the future (Pincot and Braithwaite, 2000). Many issues have been raised in this field, but the need for more studies that systematically explore the factors that affect responses to Internet-administered surveys has been noted by several authors (Couper, 2000; Pincot and Braithwaite, 2000; Smith, 1997; Strauss, 1996). Pincot and Braithwaite, for example, comment that 'there is no substitute for experimentation and live field trials as techniques are evolved to take advantage of the Internet for conducting research, which is going to be the pattern and future shape of market research' (2000: 137).

Within the behavioural and social sciences emphasis has differed somewhat. Large generalisable samples are not always what is required. As noted in Chapter 3, a growing body of literature that reports studies conducted using the Internet is emerging in social and behavioural research journals, thus demonstrating the impact of the Internet upon social science research procedures. Yet, also noted in Chapter 3, there are still very few studies that set out systematically to explore the validity of Internet procedures, compared with traditional data collection methods (for exceptions see Buchanan and Smith, 1999b; Davis, 1999). Here we consider some of the main empirical findings that have been reported and are relevant to design issues in Internet-administered survey research, from both marketing, behavioural, and social researchers. We discuss Internet-user characteristics, response rates, presentation format, confidentiality, access control, and technical issues. We then outline the options available to the researcher who wants to conduct an Internet survey, highlight the pros and cons associated with different methods, and offer a set of recommendations for good survey design.

Internet-user characteristics As discussed in Chapter 3, an issue of concern has been the extent to which Internet users differ from non-Internet users. Internet sampling procedures have been discussed extensively in that chapter. The problems with trusting data from Internet user surveys have already been outlined, and studies that compare the demographics of Internet and non-Internet samples were presented, with the conclusion that the Internet appears to enable access to larger and more diverse samples. Further evidence concerning Internet-user characteristics is available, and has implications for choices about Internet sampling procedures in survey research. Pincot and Braithwaite (2000) have suggested that more frequent Internet users are likely to be over-represented in Web surveys, and cite evidence that even moderate Internet users show dependency or 'pathological' characteristics (Griffiths, 1999). Such characteristics need to be carefully considered in relation to specific research projects, and, as we have already emphasised, the sampling technique employed will clearly influence the type of participants obtained. If Internet addiction is a real phenomenon, then the technique of placing a survey on a web site and waiting for volunteers to arrive and participate is most likely to result in over-representation of addicts and frequent users. This lends further support to our argument that alternative methods (as outlined in Chapter 3) are preferable. Posting a participation call to newsgroups or contacting individuals via their email boxes gives the researcher more control over the nature of the sample obtained, and is likely to help reduce biases due to factors likes volunteer effects and frequent-user effects. Comparison of the effects of using different Internet sampling procedures is something that is in need of further empirical research. In the meantime there will inevitably be some uncertainty about the type of sample that will be accessed by various procedures. We suggest that it is good practice to collect information on respondents' demographics, and any other characteristics that may be relevant to the study at hand and that can be easily obtained.

Response rates   Researchers often want to maximise response rates. Several studies have reported response rates for Internet surveys (for example, Mehta and Sivadas, 1995; Schillewaert et al., 1998; Tse, 1998). These reports have varied greatly, and the lack of consistency in findings is likely due to the wide variation of factors across these studies. Sheehan and McMillan (1999) review some of the studies comparing email survey response rates with those of postal surveys and note email survey response rates ranging from 6 per cent (Tse et al., 1995) to 75 per cent (Kiesler and Sproull, 1986). Smith (1997) compared two types of email survey approaches with a Web-administered survey. The email survey was either emailed directly to participants, or preceded by an emailed participation request. The latter procedure generated an overall response rate of 13.3 per cent, while the former procedure generated a response rate of 8 per cent and received one complaint that accused the researcher of spamming. We suggest that sending an initial participation request is good practice in relation to ethical codes (and 'netiquette'), as well as having the advantage of increasing response rates. The Web survey participation request was posted to a range of related interest newsgroups and resulted in 99 responses. It is not possible to measure how many people saw the request with this methodology, but Smith estimated that it would have been viewed by approximately 8,000 users. This gives a response rate of about 1.25 per cent.

In general the evidence suggests that email survey participation requests gain higher actual response rates than Web-posted surveys. However, given the sheer number of users who are likely to be exposed to a Web-posted survey, large samples can be obtained even with low response rates. The main concern with the Web-based procedure is non-response bias and lack of a sampling frame. For this reason we recommend the email request approach. Posting to newsgroups may be a more convenient alternative for some projects and does allow some estimation of sampling frame and response rates. Since a newsgroup posting will move down the list of postings fairly quickly, and will eventually expire, re-posting the request is essential in order to increase response rates. However, care should be taken not to bombard newsgroups with persistent repeated postings, and to avoid 'spamming'. Smith (1997) noted that in her study, response rate peaked immediately subsequent to a newsgroup posting. Coomber (1997a) suggests that re-posting to newsgroups once a week is appropriate.

Presentation format   There is very little research on the effects of different presentation formats in Internet-mediated survey research. Some evidence has been presented that questionnaire length is an issue that can affect response rates (Smith, 1997).[4] In our own experience of reviewing a range of Web surveys (through participation) this factor is crucial. Internet surveys are more time-consuming than paper and pencil versions by virtue of the medium. Also, it is plausible that Net users may be less inclined to spend a long time completing a Web survey due to the temptation to go and explore other pages on the Web. We found many Web surveys to be fairly lengthy, for example Likert scales with in excess of 100 items were not uncommon. One survey notified the potential respondent that the survey involved six questionnaires and would take up to two hours to complete! We wondered how many respondents actually went on to complete the survey after reading this. We would certainly expect survey length to be an important factor in influencing Internet survey response rates, and predict that future research will likely identify this as a feature on which Internet and traditional surveys differ (traditional survey research lacks conclusive evidence on survey-length effects). We recommend keeping time demands on participants within a reasonable level in order to maximise data validity.

Further issues that emerge are whether users may respond differently depending on factors such as the use of pull-down menus (which display only one option initially) as opposed to use of radio buttons (where all choices are displayed initially). Similar issues have been considered in relation to traditional survey research, but new features emerge in an IMR context. Our advice to the researcher, while awaiting these empirical clarifications, is to strive for simple, clear layouts that closely resemble paper survey formats, and to pilot and modify the survey instrument in order to test for factors like consistency between different browser formats. Another piece of advice is to make sure the survey appears as professional and well planned, with explicit affiliation with a respected institution (such as a university). The potential threat to well-designed high-quality survey research posed by the mass of data-gathering activities on the Web has been highlighted (Couper, 2000). In this climate it is particularly important for behavioural and social researchers to present their surveys as well-designed pieces of research carried out by professional academics addressing important issues.

Confidentiality   Coomber (1997a) has raised the issue of respondents' concerns about anonymity and confidentiality, especially when dealing with sensitive topics or illegal practices. In his survey research on illicit drug dealers he found that users were concerned about their responses being obtained by people other than the researcher. Several options are available that avoid users' contact details being passed on to the researcher. While email responses will typically carry the respondent's email address in the reply,[5] filling in a Web-based form will not. If respondents are still concerned about confidentiality, they can be encouraged to complete the survey on an anonymous machine (for example, in a library or Internet café) or to print it off and post it (Coomber, 1997a). Kaye and Johnson (1999) report that in a survey on attitudes to political information on the Web, 276 out of 306 respondents complied in giving their email address details, suggesting that, in some cases at least, anonymity is not a major concern to respondents.

Access control   Stanton (1998) has raised concerns about the effects of access control in Web-based surveys, suspecting that attempts to control the sampling frame by requiring participants to, for example, enter a password to access a survey page may arouse concerns about anonymity and confidentiality. This may then lead to reduced response rates, or reduced candidness. To date there is no research to suggest that this effect occurs. Whereas Stanton urges researchers to assume, for now, that implementing access control does reduce response rates and candidness, we would encourage social and behavioural researchers to aim to maximise control over who participates in the study. As argued throughout this book, keeping track of who has had the opportunity to participate in the study, that is, being able to measure the sampling frame, is essential in learning more about factors such as response rate and non-response bias in IMR. Given current concerns about the skewed demographics of the Internet-user population, such control is vitally important. Kaye and Johnson (1999) share our view that unrestricted access in Web surveys should be avoided, suggesting that passwords provide a useful method for restricting access to a select and measurable sample.

Technical issues   Some researchers have noted particular technical difficulties, which are worth documenting here in order that the reader can be aware of similar problems in his or her own research and take measures to guard against these. Smith (1997) reports that using the 'mailto:' command in the survey form in order to send responses directly to the researcher's email address, caused a problem in that the Microsoft Internet Explorer browser did not support this command. This meant that respondents using this browser were unable to submit their responses. There would also be problems if the browser was not correctly configured to send mail, for example because its SMTP server address was incorrect. Another problem reported by Smith (1997) concerned the

'Thankyou' pop-up box (implemented using JavaScript) failing to appear when the respondent pressed the 'Submit' button, resulting in multiple submissions of the same data set being sent as the user tried repeated submissions. The latter problem is something that might occur if the user has JavaScript disabled in his or her browser. As recommended in previous chapters, we suggest minimising reliance on more advanced procedures where feasible. For more complex presentations that do rely on such features it may be useful to specify these requirements in an introductory paragraph, though this must also be weighed up with the possible effect of discouraging some users by sounding too technical. Some users may have never heard of JavaScript, for example, while still using a JavaScript-enabled browser. Careful piloting should be undertaken to avoid such technical difficulties.

We recommend the use of server-side scripts (these are explained in detail below) as a method of data collection and storage. There are several reasons for this: first, problems with browsers not supporting 'mailto:' are avoided; second, users' email addresses are not automatically sent back with their data (a barrier to full anonymity); third, responses can be directed to a file, sent to an email address, or both; and, finally, many browsers pop up a warning about security when the 'mailto:' command is invoked, which may discourage some users from submitting their responses. We also emphasise the importance of thorough piloting across different platforms to check that the survey works as intended.[6]

Internet Survey Design Principles

To summarise the above discussion, we conclude with a list of ten general design principles for use in developing an Internet survey. Further research is needed to clarify and extend these principles, as well as to identify how they interact with different research goals and approaches.

1 Collect information about participant demographics (gender, education, income, nationality, occupation, and frequency of Internet use have been highlighted).
2 Aim for sampling procedures that allow measurement of sampling frame and response rates.
3 Control access to the survey (for example, by use of passwords).
4 Send a preliminary request for participation prior to sending the survey itself.
5 Include an introduction to the survey that gives affiliation details, and aim to maintain a professional appearance.
6 Aim for simplicity and clarity in layout and presentation.

7   Keep procedures and software requirements as low-tech as is poss-
    ible given the nature of the study.
8   Undertake extensive piloting across different platforms.
9   Maintain participant anonymity unless it is essential to the study to
    obtain participant identity information.
10 Use server-side scripting (as opposed to the 'mailto:' command) in
    order to collect data if resources allow.

Additional features of Internet-based surveys seem intuitively desirable. Participant tracking and honesty are issues that potentially pose a
particular problem for Internet-mediated surveys. In addition to the
principles mentioned above, further procedures can help in addressing
these issues. Participant timing is useful since particularly long or short
response times may suggest that the responses are not accurate or
genuine. Time and date stamps attached to each data submission may
help identify multiple responses from the same user, especially along
with browser and host information. Such procedures give the researcher
more confidence in being able to assess factors such as honesty and
uniqueness of responses.

In summary, a range of factors need to be taken into account in
designing an Internet survey, and design decisions should be motivated
by the features and goals of the particular piece of research. The research
question, target population, resources available, and expertise levels (of
both researcher and participants), among other factors, will need to be
considered. We now discuss exactly how Internet survey procedures,
incorporating the above recommendations, can be implemented.

Software Procedures for Implementing Internet Surveys

Email Surveys   *Simple text-based email surveys*

Implementing a simple email survey requires little technological expertise, and can be done with minimal software requirements. In its simplest
form an email survey can consist in simply sending an email containing
text questions in the body, and asking participants to hit the 'Reply'
button on their mailer, fill in their text answers to the questions, then hit
'Send' to return the completed survey questionnaire to the researcher's
email account.[7] This procedure was used by Hewson (1994), who administered an experimental questionnaire-based study via email to investigate the folk psychological concept of belief. The procedure very simply
consisted in pasting the text (which included a short story followed by a
question) into the body of an email message and sending this to
participants. Participants responded by sending back an email that
included their answer to the question.

There are many advantages in the email survey methodology. Perhaps the most salient, for many researchers, is the ease and lack of technical expertise required. This will not only prove useful for the non-computer expert researcher, but also increase the pool of available participants. A disadvantage may be the lack of control over response format. Hewson (1994) found that respondents replied in a variety of formats. Most included the question materials with their answer below, but some just sent back the answer, which would have caused problems if details of the condition sent to each participant had not been recorded. This was something that had not been anticipated.

As already discussed, when sending surveys by email the researcher needs to first obtain the participant's email address. The different ways in which this can be done have been discussed in Chapter 3. We recommended techniques that maximise knowledge of the sampling frame, as opposed to using large commercially available lists of email addresses. Hewson (1994) posted participation calls to several newsgroups, asking interested parties to reply to an email address indicating that they would like to take part in the study, or requesting further information. This methodology was considered successful in that it generated 135 responses within a period of approximately two weeks. Response rates were not able to be measured in this case because it was not known how many people had seen the request. The issues of dormant accounts, accounts that are checked infrequently, and users with multiple accounts were also raised. These issues are less likely to be problematic for methods that access respondents from newsgroups (either by posting a request, or obtaining email addresses from postings) than for methods that use large lists of harvested email addresses. Nevertheless, further techniques can be employed to try to avoid some of these problems, which still may occur. Sending a receipt request (an option on several mailers, for example, Netscape communicator) can be useful in helping determine whether the user has actually opened the email message, though a returned receipt cannot guarantee that the message has actually been read, and lack of a returned receipt certainly does not warrant the conclusion that the message has not been read (users can reject receipt requests). The method of posting participation requests on web pages, inviting interested parties to respond by email, is also a possibility, but we have discouraged this general approach due to the problem of lack of knowledge of the sampling frame (though a number of researchers have piloted ways of keeping track of web site visitors, and this approach could become viable in the future).

While quick and easy to implement, the text-based email survey methodology does have drawbacks. First, the limitation to text-based materials makes it unsuitable for some types of research that require more sophisticated graphics. Much survey research is text-based, but even implementing something like a Likert-type response scale is likely to be ungainly via text-based email, as compared with an HTML form, for example. A further consideration with this method is that anonymity is not preserved since emails can be traced to individuals by the header with sender address information. (As mentioned previously, anonymous email services are available, but relying on this technique will place additional demands on respondents and thus limit the accessible respondent pool.) In sum, a text-based email approach in IMR may work well in some cases but prove too limited in others.

Email-based surveys with graphics   Moving beyond email surveys that use only text, there are several possibilities available. One procedure is to email a file as an attachment, which can contain graphics. The participant can open and edit this and send back to the researcher. Most users will have the required skills to open file attachments, which is particularly straightforward on Windows-based systems, for example. However, platform variation may limit accessibility and participation: different platforms, for example Windows, UNIX, will be able to handle different file formats. This issue needs to be carefully considered. HTML files can be sent as email attachments, and mailers such as Netscape communicator will automatically display these as HTML documents in the body of the email message. Thus if an HTML form (like the type described in the previous chapter, and further elaborated below) is sent, users will simply be able to respond to this form within their browser in the same way that they would respond to a WWW form online. The recipient will simply fill in the form and click the 'Submit' button while connected to the Internet, which will return the data to a script on the researcher's server (which will then save the data to file or mail it to the researcher). The approach reduces the effort required by the participant, compared with having to open and edit a file, then email this back to the researcher.

Thus email can be used to send anything from very simple text questions, to sophisticated HTML forms that are processed by a server script. The latter approach allows the most flexibility and sophistication, and we now turn to discuss how to construct such a form and place it on a web server, bearing in mind that it is equally feasible, and in many cases more desirable (for reasons already discussed), to control who receives the form by sending it via email.[8]

WWW Surveys

Creating a simple Web-based survey is actually not that difficult. The reader can use the code given here in order to produce the survey (HTML form) itself, and should have little difficulty in modifying this survey to fit his or her own requirements, with reference to the useful resources on HTML provided (see 'resources' at the end of this chapter). Placing the survey on a suitable server may require more skill, or help from technical staff. However, once this modest barrier has been crossed, it should be easy to produce further surveys and place these on the server in a similar manner.[9] To produce a program that inputs the data received directly into an analysis package (such as SPSS) requires more programming expertise, and we do not cover this here. Some readers may find commercially available survey construction packages useful, though these are costly and tend to be aimed particularly at market researchers. We found many such commercial packages available, through an online search. These are some of them (found during February 2001): Survey Said survey software (*www.surveysaid.com*); Perseus Survey Solutions software (*www.perseus.com/*); Web Surveyor (*www.websurveyor.com/home_intro.asp*). A further problem with these packages is the restrictions on being able fully to customise forms and data collection in the way the researcher wants. Similar resources are starting to be developed by social and behavioural researchers, however, and some of these are fairly useful (though still in the developmental phase, or otherwise rather limited in terms of sophistication and flexibility). Examples are WWW survey assistant (*OR.Psychology.Dal.Ca/~wcs/hidden/Sadocs*) and SurveyWiz (*psych.fullerton.edu/mbirnbaum/programs/surveyWiz.htm#top*). Such packages are discussed in more detail in Chapter 6. Some authors refer to Polyform software, published by O'Reilly and Associates (for example, Birnbaum, 2001), but unfortunately this program was discontinued as of 18 January 2001.

Implementing a WWW Survey

This section demonstrates how to set up a simple survey using HTML forms and collect the data using a basic server-side script, then introduces a few JavaScript techniques with which the survey page can be enhanced. The survey page should work with any modern browser, and we describe server scripts that will work on an appropriately configured UNIX server and on a Windows server. While no experience with HTML is required to get the survey page working, no explanation of the non-form elements is given here. Readers who wish to learn more about HTML should look elsewhere, in any of the many books and online sites dedicated to the subject (like those listed at the end of this chapter).

The Survey Page

The essential component of any HTML survey is a form. Figure 5.1 shows an example survey page using a form, displayed in a browser.

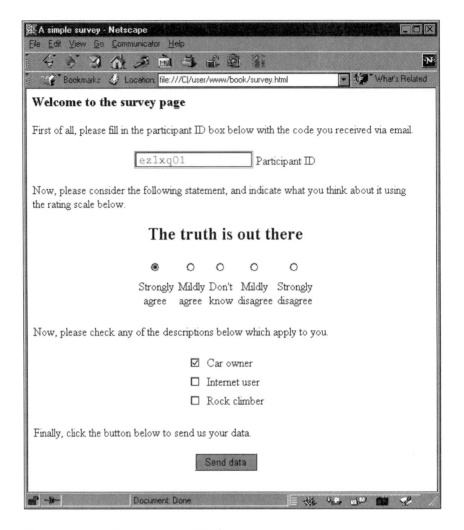

Figure 5.1 *A simple survey, using HTML forms*

Figure 5.2 shows the underlying HTML code used to generate it; the code uses text, radio, and checkbox elements to create the onscreen interface devices. The reader is encouraged to type this code into a text editor, to create a file that can be loaded into a web browser. Use a filename like 'survey.html', save it in plain text format, and load it into a browser to see how it looks.[10]

Looking at the HTML code in Figure 5.2, the form dominates the page, although there is significant use of tables to format form elements. The first form element to be used is the text input box, which just allows users to type in a short line of text – in this case it is used to gather

```
<html>
<head>
<title>A simple survey</title>
</head>
<body>
<h1>Welcome to the survey page</h1>

<form name=myform method=post action="mailto:scully@fbi.gov">

<p>First of all, please fill in the participant ID box below
with the code you received via email.</p>

<center><p><input type=text name=userid> Participant ID</p>
</center>

<p>Now, please consider the following statement, and indicate
what you think about it using the rating scale below.</p>

<h2 align=center>The truth is out there</h2>

<table align=center>
<tr>
<td align=center><input type=radio name=truth value=2></td>
<td align=center><input type=radio name=truth value=1></td>
<td align=center><input type=radio name=truth value=0></td>
<td align=center><input type=radio name=truth value=-1></td>
<td align=center><input type=radio name=truth value=-2></td>
</tr>
<tr>
<td align=center>Strongly<br>agree</td>
<td align=center>Mildly<br>agree</td>
<td align=center>Don't<br>know</td>
<td align=center>Mildly<br>disagree</td>
<td align=center>Strongly<br>disagree</td>
</tr>
</table>

<p>Now, please check any of the descriptions below which apply
to you.</p>

<table align=center>
<tr><td><input type=checkbox name=carowner></td><td>Car owner
</td></tr>
<tr><td><input type=checkbox name=netuser></td><td>Internet
user</td></tr>
<tr><td><input type=checkbox name=climber></td><td>Rock climber
</td></tr>
</table>

<p>Finally, click the button below to send us your data.</p>
<center><input type=submit value="Send data"></center>
</form> </body>
```

Figure 5.2 *HTML to define a form for a simple survey*

participant ID codes. Next, there is an example of the use of multiple radio elements to implement a rating scale; participants are asked to rate their agreement with a proposition, by clicking on one of a set of radio elements. All the radio elements that share the same name are bound together, and clicking on one clears all the rest, so at most only one is selected at one time. This behaviour is ideal for implementing a discrete rating scale.

After the truth question, there is a series of independent checkboxes to allow participants to answer a series of yes/no questions by simply ticking the boxes that apply to them.

At the bottom of the page is the 'Send data' button, which, when clicked, should cause the data that has been entered into the rest of the form to be sent somewhere (specified in the main FORM tag's ACTION parameter). If you actually click this button, your browser will attempt to send an email to *scully@fbi.gov*, containing your responses to the questionnaire. More usefully perhaps, you could try replacing the email address with your own, and as long as your browser is appropriately configured to send email, when you click the button, you will send yourself email. It is obvious how this method can be used to gather data: simply mail the HTML file to respondents as an HTML attachment, and ask them to complete the form and click the button to return the data to you. While this may prove to be effective, still, as described above, it does not work if the respondent's browser is incorrectly configured, for example.

The next section shows how you can make this simple HTML form interact with a script on a web server, to provide an alternative way of gathering data.

A Simple UNIX Server Script

To make your HTML form send its data somewhere other than your email account for collection, you need to make use of a proper web server. Most probably you will create a directory inside your server's directory space and copy your survey.html file in there. Then it will be accessible via the server, using a URL such as *myserver.tld/mysurvey/ survey.html*. To make the survey work properly in this context, you should replace the ACTION = "mailto:scully@fbi.gov" option with ACTION = "savedata.cgi", where 'savedata.cgi' is a file in the same directory on the server as 'survey.html'. This section describes a way to create this file.

The Common Gateway Interface (CGI) is a way for web server programs to use arbitrary programs on the server machine to process incoming data from forms. On UNIX servers, this can be any program,

```
#!/bin/sh

cat>>datafile

echo>>datafile

cat<<EOF

content-type: text/html

<HTML>

<HEAD><TITLE>Acknowledgement</TITLE></HEAD>

<BODY>

<H3>Thank you for sending the data. The experiment is over.</H3>

</BODY>

</HTML>
```

Figure 5.3   *A simple CGI script for a UNIX server to save submitted data to file and display an acknowledgement message to the user*

written in any of a wide range of ordinary programming languages such as Perl, C, or whatever you like. Figure 5.3 shows an example of a script which can be run on a UNIX server to save incoming form data to a single file, and then return an acknowledgement message to the client browser. Again, the reader is encouraged to type in the program code, and save it as 'savedata.cgi' in the same directory as 'survey.html'.

The script specifies its command interpreter (in this case, the default UNIX shell, /bin/sh), then uses this to append the standard input (the raw data stream from the client) to the data file (called 'datafile'). The 'echo' command appends a new line character so each record begins on a new line. The remainder of the script then just sends an embedded HTML acknowledgement message back to the client on the standard output. When a form is submitted using this file as its ACTION, the web server software will attempt to execute this program. This means its execute permission must be set appropriately – ask your webmaster for appropriate settings for your web server. Also, your webmaster may or may not permit executing CGI programs within ordinary user space – you may be required to relocate the savedata.cgi program to a directory like /cgi-bin/ Finally, you will need to create the file 'datafile' in the same directory as savedata.cgi, and give it suitable write permissions (ask your webmaster how to do this) to allow the server process to write to the file.

Assuming you get all this to work, when you load the survey page from the server in your browser, answer the questions, and click the 'Send data' button, then your data will be sent to the server and saved to the datafile, and the acknowledgement message should appear in your browser window.

If you take a look at the datafile contents using a text editor, you should see one or more lines like this:

    userid=ezlxq01&truth=2&netuser=on

Each data record is in the form of a series of <variablename=value> pairs, corresponding to the form elements, and separated by '&' characters. You will also notice that only those checkboxes that have been checked by the user are included; unchecked checkboxes are just ignored. Other codes may be apparent if other types of input are used: if text contains spaces, these will be replaced by '+' characters, and any non-alphanumeric characters will be expressed as a pair of hexadecimal digits preceded by a '%' character. This data format is known as URL-encoded, and it will need to be cleaned up a little before analysis, but this can easily be achieved with a text editor.

It is easy to modify the script to send data to your email account, if required. Provided your UNIX server is configured to send email, you can replace the two lines

    cat >> datafile
    echo >> datafile

with a single line like this:

    mail mulder@fbi.gov

Obviously you need to use your own email address here, rather than the fictional agent's. Then each form submission will be sent to your email account individually, instead of being saved to file. This may be more appropriate for some purposes. Indeed it may be useful to use both methods concurrently. This method has the same result as the 'mailto:' method described above, but without the dependence on the respondent's browser settings.

Scripts like these are fully general, in that they can handle arbitrary form submissions using the POST method, so you may not need any more server-side scripting if you're happy to receive your data in URL-encoded form, and you don't want the server to behave differently (that is, send out different pages) depending on form contents.

In the next section we describe the kernel of a more sophisticated method, based on parsing the values of variables out of the raw form submission, using a Windows-based scripting language. Similar techniques are also applicable to UNIX servers, with some adaptation.

An ASP-Based Windows Server Script

Many people will have access to a Microsoft Windows server, such as the Personal Information Server on Windows 98, or the Internet Information Server on Windows 2000. These servers behave similarly to UNIX-based servers, but do not encourage the use of the raw Common Gateway Interface. Instead, Windows servers offer a fairly simple but powerful system based on Active Server Pages (ASP), which allow the integration of scripting with HTML content on the server side. Both JScript (Microsoft's version of JavaScript) and VBScript are supported; we will give an example using VBScript.

As in the UNIX example above, the first step is to create a directory on your server, somewhere under the server's document root directory, called 'survey' or whatever you like, and copy the 'survey.html' file into it. You will need to set the value of the ACTION parameter of the FORM tag to 'savedata.asp'. Make sure you can access the file, using a browser pointing to a suitable URL. Next, you will need to create the 'savedata.asp' file, by copying the code in Figure 5.4 into a text editor and saving it in your survey directory under that name.

The way it works is as follows: ASP pages are interpreted by the Windows server as specifying a page to send out to the client, possibly with inline, script-generated inclusions, rather as a web page including script is interpreted on the client side. Script commands are executed as they are found, which implies that the VBScript code included in Figure 5.4 is executed before the HTML below it is sent to the client. This does not matter in the present case, but is important in more sophisticated applications.

The first line directs the server to set the default script language (included between <% and %> brackets) to be VBScript. The next portion specifies a series of inline VBScript commands, followed by a procedure definition. The procedure, named 'saveData', with two arguments, is called once by the inline commands, and its function is to append as a single record, the string given as its second argument to the file whose name is specified as the first argument.

The inline code defines two variables, and initialises one of them as an array of variable names, and the other as an empty string. Then, for each of the variable names, its associated value is recovered from the FORM submission, and a term composed of the name and the value is added to the developing string, which will eventually represent the entire form submission for this page. When, finally, all variable values have been added to the string, the whole string is written as a record to the

```
<%@language="VBScript"%>

<%
  Dim thevars,thestring
  thevars=Array)"pid","truth","carowner","netuser","climber")

  thestring=""

  For Each item In thevars

     thestring=thestring & item & "="& Request.Form(item) &" "

  Next

  saveData "datafile.txt",thestring
Sub saveData(myFile,myString)

  Const ForReading=1,ForAppending=8

  Const canCreateFile=True,cantCreateFile=False

  Const useASCII=0,useUnicode=-1

  Dim fs,f

  Set fs=CreateObject("Scripting.FileSystemObject")

  Set f=fs.OpenTextFile(myFile,ForAppending,canCreateFile,useASCII)

  f.WriteLine myString

  f.Close

End Sub

%>

<HTML>

<HEAD><TITLE>Acknowledgement</TITLE></HEAD>

<BODY>

<H3 ALIGN=center>Thank you for sending the data.<BR>The experiment
is over.</H3>

</BODY>

</HTML>
```

Figure 5.4   *A simple ASP page for a Microsoft Windows server, to save submitted data to file and display an acknowledgement message to the user*

specified file, using the 'saveData' procedure, and then the script portion exits, leaving the server to output the HTML inclusions, at the bottom of the file, to the client.

If your form submits variables whose names do not appear on the list of declared variables specified in the script, you will need to update the list, or else unmentioned variables' values will be ignored. If you want to submit the form using METHOD=GET, you need to replace instances of 'Request.Form(item)' with 'Request.QueryString(item)'. The exact way in which the file in the 'saveData' procedure is opened depends on values given to the second, third, and fourth arguments of the 'OpenTextFile' method; these use constants specified at the beginning of the procedure, and you can experiment with them if you like.

The ASP file seems to execute, by default, in the root directory on the main drive, that is, C:\, so it writes the data file to this directory. You will probably want to put the data file somewhere else; to do this, you can give an absolute file specification as the first argument to the procedure, such as 'c:\my\directory\datafile.txt'.

With this type of solution, you can easily change the outputs of the ASP file depending on the submitted values; it just depends on your ability to program in the selected scripting language. A simple example is all we will provide here: add the following lines after the one containing the <BODY> tag in the ASP example:

```
<% If (Request.Form("truth") < 0) then %>
  <H3 ALIGN=center>You may be the Cancer Man</H3>
<% Elseif (Request.Form("truth") > 0) then %>
  <H3 ALIGN=center>You are as bad as Mulder</H3>
<% End If %>
```

Now you will find that when the participant submits the main form, the final page makes an uncomplimentary comment, based on the participant's response to the 'truth' question. This type of behaviour can be very useful (although not usually for taunting respondents) – see Microsoft's server documentation for more details on ASP pages and server-side scripting on Microsoft machines. Similar facilities are available on UNIX if you use Perl or other scripting languages.

Adding JavaScript to the HTML Form

Incorporating JavaScript in HTML documents is quite easy, and can add many useful features to your pages. You should note that not every browser supports JavaScript, and even though most do, not everyone will have it enabled, so you need to consider what happens when it is disabled. Sometimes, the system can still work without the functions you added; this approach is to be recommended if possible.

Getting More Information

It can be useful to know what type of browser the participant is using. You can get this information using JavaScript, if it is enabled. We use it to write a small amount of HTML code to the page as it is being loaded (the JavaScript executes inline), to define a hidden form element containing a string that describes the browser in use. When the form is submitted, this extra information is sent to the server along with all the rest.

Somewhere inside the form definition in the survey example, for example after the line '<form name=myform method=post ...>', add the following lines:

```
<script language=javascript>
document.writeln('<input type=hidden name=browser value=
"'+navigator.userAgent+'">');
</script>
```

Now, when you load the page, an extra hidden form element should be created. This is not visible onscreen, but you can check it is there by viewing the source code for the browser window.

If the user has disabled JavaScript, the code within the <script> tag will be ignored, so the hidden form element will not be created and the server will not get any information about the browser, but this is unlikely to be critical in this case – everything else should work as before. If JavaScript is enabled, you will get information about the browser type and version, and the operating system on which it is running.

You can use a similar trick to get the URL of the referring page – the page containing the link that the user clicked to arrive at your page. Before the '</script>' line, add another line of JavaScript to define another hidden form element, like this:

```
document.writeln('<input type=hidden name=referrer value=
"'+document.referrer+'">');
```

You should note that the referrer will only be defined if the user reached your page by clicking on a link on another page, otherwise the referrer string will be empty.

Knowing the referrer page can be very helpful if you have advertised your survey page in several different locations, since it can allow you to discover how many of your participants have arrived via each of the links. Note, though, that if this is the way you have advertised your survey, potential participants will not have received an ID code, so you will not want to ask them for one. Also, you will not get any useful information if you interpose a page before the one containing the survey form, for instructions or whatever, since then all you will get is the URL of the instruction page.

If you have looked at the datafile records returned by these hidden elements, you will have noticed that the browser and referrer information seem garbled, with strange intrusions, perhaps looking something like this:

browser=Mozilla%2F4.5+%5Ben%5D+%28X11%3B+I%3B+Linux
+2.0.35+i586%29

This is because the strings contain non-alphabetic characters, which are expressed in hexadecimal codes in URL-encoded format. Despite this, you can probably decipher enough to retrieve the information you need: for example, the above record indicates that the browser is Mozilla (that is, Netscape Navigator), English language version 4.5, running under the X11 windowing system on Linux version 2.0.35 on an Intel 586 (Pentium) processor.

Timing Participants

A slightly more complex example demonstrates how you can obtain crude timings, in this case the time taken by the participant to complete the survey, from the point at which the page has been fully displayed, until the moment they click the 'Send data' button.

First of all, we need to define a hidden form element that will contain the time value when the form is submitted. There is no need to do this in JavaScript, so just add the following line of HTML somewhere inside the form:

```
<input type=hidden name=time value="">
```

Next we define a pair of functions, one of which is used to start the timer, and the other of which is used to stop it. These must be defined somewhere convenient, and for this sort of thing it is conventional to put the code, enclosed in <script> . . . </script> tags, in the header of the document, just before the </head> tag.

```
<script language=javascript>

function startTimer()
{
    beginTime=new Date();
}
```

```
function stopTimer()
{
    endTime=new Date();
    document.myform.time.value=endTime-beginTime;
    return true;
}
```

</script>

Notice that the 'stopTimer()' function actually modifies the value of the hidden form element called 'time', before the form is submitted.

Finally, we need to call these functions at appropriate points. We can start the timer when the page has finished loading by replacing the <body> tag with

```
<body onLoad="startTimer()">
```

Similarly, we can add a handler to the <form> tag to tell it to call the 'stopTimer()' function when the participant clicks the 'Send data' button, like this:

```
<form name=myform method=post action=savedata.cgi onSubmit=
"return stopTimer()">
```

If this is all set up properly, the time taken by the participant to complete the survey form (in milliseconds) will be sent back to the server when the 'Send data' button is clicked. If JavaScript is disabled, the system should still work, but the time value returned to the server will be empty.

Form Data Validation

As the reader may have discovered by now, when the 'Send data' button is clicked, no testing occurs to ensure that form elements have been filled in, checked, or selected; it is quite easy for participants to supply no information at all and just submit an empty form. Happily, it is possible to use JavaScript to check that the form really has been filled in before allowing it to be submitted.

To check that the participant ID box has been filled in, you can add the following code before the final line in the 'stopTimer()' function (that is, just before 'return true').

```
if (document.myform.userid.value =="")
{
    alert('Please enter your participant ID');
    return false;
}
```

The effect of this is to check whether the participant ID box is empty, and if so, to pop up an alert dialogue box to remind the participant to fill it in, and to prevent the form being submitted to the server. If the participant ID is not empty, the 'stopTimer()' function should return the Boolean value 'true', allowing form submission to go ahead.

The 'stopTimer()' function now has a new role, to test for the validity of form data, as well as recording timings. You might like to change its name to reflect its new status, to something like 'handleSubmit()', and of course you should remember to update the reference to it in the <FORM> tag too.

It is still possible to submit the form without having answered the question about the truth. Tackling this is slightly more complicated, since in this case we want to ensure that one of the boxes comprising the rating scale has been checked. This implies the use of more complex code, so it is convenient to define a general function, which will allow us to re-use the same code with every radio object we might define in future. To do this, add the following function somewhere in the main JavaScript section:

```
function testRadio(objradio)
{
    is_checked=false;
    for (i=0; i < objradio.length; i++)
        if (objradio[i].checked)
        {
            is_checked=true;
            break;
        }
    return is_checked;
}
```

The function will return 'true' if any member of the radio complex (whose name is to be supplied as the argument of the function) has been checked, otherwise it will return 'false'. Now, to perform the actual test and pop up the alert box if required, add the following code after the participant ID check, but before the final 'return true':

```
if (!testRadio(document.myform.truth))
    {
        alert('Please tell us what you think of the truth sentence');
        return false;
    }
```

The exclamation mark preceding the function call specifies logical negation, so if the test does not return 'true', the alert box will be popped up to prompt the participant, and the form will not be submitted until the next time the participant clicks the 'Send data' button. At this point, all the testing will be repeated, until the form is finally completed and the function returns 'true', allowing the data to be submitted to the server.

Since the remaining checkboxes on the form are strictly optional, there is no need to test them. The above code will work if JavaScript is enabled on the client, but even if it is disabled, the form should still function and be submitted as usual. In this event, there will be no data validation, as was the case before we added the testing code.

Stimulus Randomisation

It is a common requirement in experimental studies and surveys that biases inherent in materials should be eliminated where possible. In the present case, an obvious potential for bias exists in the form of the truth question, namely the constant left–right order of the rating scale response alternatives. Perhaps participants tend to click the leftmost box, irrespective of the sense of the question; in case this is so, we can control against it by presenting the response scale in either of two orders, randomly, then we can expect any such directional biases to cancel out statistically.

Since, as we have already seen, we can use JavaScript inline, we can replace the ordinary HTML code used to generate the truth rating scale, and use JavaScript's built-in random number function to write the rating scale forwards or backwards on a random basis. You can make this work by replacing the lines between '<table align=center><tr>' and '</tr></table>' with the following code:

```
<script language=javascript>
if (Math.random() < 0.5)
{
    document.writeln('<td align=center><input type=radio name=truth
    value=2></td>');
    document.writeln('<td align=center><input type=radio name=truth
    value=1></td>');
    document.writeln('<td align=center><input type=radio name=truth
    value=0></td>');
    document.writeln('<td align=center><input type=radio name=truth
    value=-1></td>');
    document.writeln('<td align=center><input type=radio name=truth
    value=-2></td>');
    document.writeln('</tr>');
    document.writeln('<tr>');
    document.writeln('<td align=center>Strongly<br>agree</td>');
    document.writeln('<td align=center>Mildly<br>agree</td>');
    document.writeln('<td align=center>Don't<br>know</td>');
    document.writeln('<td align=center>Mildly<br>disagree</td>');
    document.writeln('<td align=center>Strongly<br>disagree</td>');
```

```
} else {
    document.writeln('<td align=center><input type=radio name=truth
    value=-2></td>');
    document.writeln('<td align=center><input type=radio name=truth
    value=-1></td>');
    document.writeln('<td align=center><input type=radio name=truth
    value=0></td>');
    document.writeln('<td align=center><input type=radio name=truth
    value=1></td>');
    document.writeln('<td align=center><input type=radio name=truth
    value=2></td>');
    document.writeln('</tr>');
    document.writeln('<tr>');
    document.writeln('<td align=center>Strongly<br>disagree</td>');
    document.writeln('<td align=center>Mildly<br>disagree</td>');
    document.writeln('<td align=center>Don't<br>know</td>');
    document.writeln('<td align=center>Mildly<br>agree</td>');
    document.writeln('<td align=center>Strongly<br>agree</td>');
}
</script>
```

This code replaces the literal HTML code with inline JavaScript 'document.writeln()' statements in both possible orders, and makes use of the built-in function 'Math.random()', which returns a random value between 0 and 1, to decide which one actually gets displayed. It is left to the reader, as an exercise, to find a way to tell the server which random order has been selected in any particular case.

Unlike our previous JavaScript examples, this one does not degrade gracefully on browsers where JavaScript is disabled, or otherwise not available; in fact it will not display any rating scale at all in these circumstances. However, in this case it is easy to supply a default HTML version for display in case scripting is unavailable: just include the original HTML code for the non-randomised version, enclosed between <NOSCRIPT> . . . </NOSCRIPT> tags, after the final </SCRIPT> tag. This piece of code will only be displayed if scripting is unavailable, so in such cases at least an unrandomised version will be displayed, and the methods described above should be sufficient to detect afterwards whether scripting was available or not.

Conclusion

Building on techniques described in this chapter, it should be a straight-forward matter for someone with modest HTML skills to implement simple Web-based surveys, returning the data to a central server for storage. As well as giving examples showing how to construct a survey form, and a server script to collect and store the data, we have shown how to use JavaScript to exploit extra data sources such as timings, browser versions, and referrer URLs, and how to enhance the interface to encourage full reporting by the participant and to control against materials biases.

If you want to learn more, there are a number of online resources[11] devoted to development of online surveys and experiments, although we take no responsibility for the content of these sites:

M. Birnbaum, SurveyWiz: *psych.fullerton.edu/mbirnbaum/programs/surveyWiz. htm#top*

Express: Experiment Presentation Server, for HTML/script clients, at *express. psyc.bbk.ac.uk/*

P. Kenyon, 'How to Put Questionnaires on the Internet': *salmon.psy.plym.ac.uk/ mscprm/forms.htm*

K. McGraw, PsychExps Developer's Corner: *psychexps.olemiss.edu/Developers/ index.htm*

WWW Survey Assistant: or.psychology.dal.ca/~wcs/hidden/home.html

Comprehensive documentation on HTML and JavaScript is available at *developer.netscape.com/docs/*

A list of HTML guides and tutorials can be found at: *lcweb.loc.gov/global/ internet/html.html#about*

Notes

1   A substantial body of literature on these issues is beginning to emerge within market research journals. The literature at time of writing, however, appears primarily focused on how to increase response rates in Internet surveys. A number of authors have highlighted the need for further systematic studies that examine factors that can affect Internet survey responses (for example, Couper, 2000).

2   Educational level has been one of the concerns raised in relation to Internet samples, the idea being that Net users are typically more educated than non-Net users. Perhaps, then, Net users are similar to mail survey respondents in this sense.

3   For example, the American Psychological Association's 'Psychological Research on the Net' page had 107 online studies listed on 30 August 2001. Several of these were actually links to other pages that included a number of studies.

4   Using an experimental non-survey procedure, Krantz et al. (1997) reported that of the respondents who started their Web study, 17 per cent continued to completion in one condition, whereas 29 per cent continued to completion in another condition. They pointed out that the condition with the higher completion rate had half the number of trials, and suggested that this was a likely cause of the different completion rates observed.

5   There are ways of sending email through an anonymous mailer program that will strip off the user email address details.

6   Though as Smith (1997) reports, this approach isn't foolproof, since things that appear to be working during the piloting phase can still prove to be problematic during the study phase.

7   A range of mailers are available on different platforms. Some of the most commonly used are Pegasus, Netscape communicator, Eudora (Windows), Pine, and Elm (UNIX).

8   Access to a survey residing on a webpage can also be controlled, however.

9   As we have discussed extensively in Chapter 3 and above, a range of different sampling procedures may be implemented when conducting a Web-based survey. We have recommended making initial email contact with potential participants and then directing them to the survey page, making use of passwords for participant tracking. Alternatives are possible, such as Dahlen's (1998) procedure for obtaining a probability sample in a Web-based survey, but require more technical complexity and, we have argued, are less appropriate to the behavioural and social researcher than to the market researcher.

10 Note that if saved as a Word document, then problems will emerge, in that the browser will display the text, not interpret the HTML code.

11 Note that website addresses can very quickly go out of date. At least one of the sites listed here required updating because it changed its address during the course of writing this book. However, a keyword search (using a search engine such as *www.google.com*) is a good way of locating sites that have moved.

6

What Can Go Wrong?

Although we argued in Chapter 3 that the Internet provides an effective and economical means for accessing a vast and diverse number of potential participants, Internet-based research shares with many other modes certain methodological problems relating to, for example, the participant's willingness to participate, and the nature of interactions with the researcher.[1] However, even here, Internet-based research has some crucial advantages, particularly in the way certain of these effects can be controlled for, thereby helping both to reduce the influence of these factors and to isolate the role that they play. A primary feature of IMR that contributes to the control of experimental artefacts is that Internet access can be anonymous. Research is conducted from computer accounts that can be assigned names suggesting at least gender and nationality, perhaps race as well. There are no voice or appearance effects, just the image that is conveyed through communications associated with the study – it is thus possible to manipulate the portrayed gender, race, and nationality effects in order to either reduce the role of these attributes or deliberately convey some specific attribute, depending on the nature of the research question.

This chapter outlines methods for addressing some of the issues raised. We also outline specific pitfalls that can emerge and suggest solutions, preventative and, where possible, *post hoc*. However, awareness of the potential for things to go wrong is the first step in preventing mishaps. The sorts of issues that are at stake are, among others: data loss (via corruption or transmission failures based on the technology), participant drop-out rates, and hacker vandalism. We suggest solutions that entail in the main maximal researcher control of materials and in fact all electronic communications associated with research. We outline how these considerations interact with the range of methodologies introduced in Chapter 4. That is, for each of the possible Internet-based instruments for research, we discuss how the principles of researcher control are at stake. While the theme of the chapter is the space of things that can go wrong in Internet-administered studies, the focus is on how to anticipate problems and how to recover from them when they have been unanticipated.

Equipment

It has already been pointed out that there is a basic trade-off between having Internet-based studies that test what one is interested in and having the facilities for participating in those studies generally available. The more facilities required, the fewer participants will be available with access to comparable equipment. Additionally, as a rule of thumb, the more specialised the equipment requirements, the less broad-based the participant pool. Equally, the more complex the materials used in a study, the more difficult it can be to set up the study and control the data collection. This section discusses some of the issues raised in the chapter on equipment for Internet-based research, pointing out where problems revealed there can be addressed, and where additional problems may reside.

As pointed out throughout this book, it is not essential that an Internet study be fully interactive. Case studies are reported here (see Chapter 7) that demonstrate the most basic of Internet access methods. However, for the purposes of this section, it is convenient to suppose that the researcher prefers to construct a study that makes the most of interactive text and graphics, with accessibility run through common modes of access to the Internet – web browsers like Netscape or Internet Explorer.[2] Also, we shall suppose that the researcher has implemented a study using some of the advanced programming languages discussed in Chapter 4 – HTML pages and Java and Javascript coding.

The last thing most researchers want to do is become Web programmers, and the demands of becoming proficient are actually quite substantial, with many details to attend to.[3] Some of these have been addressed already, such as maintaining proper security over the files, perhaps by issuing passwords to intended users, and monitoring logs of access. Even though facilities like the Apache server, which run under UNIX and are freely available, provide security options, the researcher must still expend a great deal of energy implementing them, in the general case. Moreover, testing is extremely important, as a study with HTML pages designed with one particular browser for the prototyping platform can easily have a vastly different behaviour when viewed from an alternative browser (or even the same browser family, but executed from a distinct hardware architecture). At any rate, in some of our work and that of our students,[4] this has been an occasional problem (McGowan, 1999). The most trivial version of the problem is for HTML pages to view in vastly different font sizes on various platforms. One can imagine this fact ruining a study if the original design depended on all of a text being visible at once, yet where some participants (without even knowing which)[5] are able to see only one small sector of the intended viewing field.

However, other browser-related points are also important to attend to. Default settings and HTML are important to avoid. One should not rely on default settings in constructing HTML but should set colours and relative font sizes as explicitly as possible. To see the importance of this, consider a study in which colour is important, and in which various colours have been placed against a default background. If participants' web browsers have different default settings, they will essentially be presented with unintended materials, materials that perhaps lack the intended effect of colour contrasts. This can be an issue even if colour contrasts are not the topic of research. Texts presented on the web page can become impossible to read when set against an ill-chosen background colour.[6] Therefore, it is important that the researcher designing web pages fill in appropriate values for defaults wherever possible.[7] We emphasise that it is advisable to test thoroughly in these respects before the study takes place.

Additionally, for the advanced Java applications to work correctly, it is necessary for the participant's browser to be set to Java-enabled mode. The very nature of Java is that it is not permitted to change the setting for the user; thus, certain participants will be eliminated by the equipment if they do not happen to be using a Java-enabled browser. (Many of these will not experience much of the study at all, therefore it is necessary to provide mechanisms that supply informative texts to those participants explaining why their experiment is not proceeding.) However, the researcher is also susceptible to subtle variations in implementations. Recently, we discovered that even Java-enabled browsers do not always behave properly – Netscape Communicator 4.7, for example, intermittently does not interpret Java programs even when Java-enabled (Timothy, 2000). Studies that rely on certain software 'plugins' are also problematic when participants lack the necessary plugin at the start of interaction. In a worst-case scenario, the need for the plugin becomes relevant only part-way through the study, but the participant's home machine lacks sufficient disk space (or has some similar constraint) to download the software, thus nullifying the participant's contribution altogether.

Researchers who are depending on accurate reaction-time data should also be aware of the foibles of measuring such data remotely. Network lags during busy times of the day may artificially inflate the amount of time participants required for particular events within the study. However, measuring those events not on the server but on the participant's home machine (using an applet) is sensitive to various hardware facts about the home machine. Essentially, it becomes a requirement to have a part of the experimental server software responsible to identify what sort of software and hardware each participant is using. This is one way to cope with some of the problems both with browser versions, and with applet-calculated timings. In any case, the accuracy of timings is a current topic of research.

More mundane issues enter the picture for researchers intending to embark on longitudinal studies given a certain degree of flux that currently exists in Internet usage patterns. In particular, many Internet users, most notably the population of university undergraduates and students generally, often have annually changing usernames and passwords. This suggests the value of running a study on a server that hosts user accounts for studies requiring longitudinal data (for these purposes, this means any study lasting more than a year, or involving sampling of the same participants for more than a year). This follows because then the user simply needs to remember an agreed account and password on the server hosting the study.[8]

However, when participants forget their passwords, and their user ID information has changed, it is non-trivial to match the participant to the correct account and password while still maintaining overall integrity of the participant's data. It becomes necessary to monitor a larger amount of personal information about the participant in those cases in order to verify continuity of the same participant under a new home user ID. Worse, though, if the longitudinal participant obtains a new account, and for whatever reason ceased to check an old account, then it becomes impossible to email participants successfully to remind them of appointments for updated participation. This said, longitudinal studies are difficult for conventional research paradigms as well.

Recently, researchers have begun developing general-purpose systems intended to accommodate many of the issues raised in this section. There are a number of software systems that can be downloaded from the Internet or used remotely.[9] For example, an extensive suite of studies is freely available at *www.olemiss.edu/projects/PsychExps/* and intended for psychology instructors to get students to participate in classic experimental designs. The site is configured to record participant data for registered users, and has facilities for monitoring reaction times. The main drawback of the system is that it presumes PC or Mac environments, and for users to contribute new studies it is necessary that they be developed using certain Authorware scripting tools. McGraw and Tew (1997) are critical of a related project, the Internet Psychology Laboratory (*kahuna.psych.uiuc.edu/ipl/*), on the basis of the fact that it does not make use of Shockwave, a freely downloadable but limited platform technology that enables multimedia studies, but uses Java instead. While their arguments about the fleetingness of many programming languages in the history of computing systems cannot be dismissed, due consideration is not given to the fact that many programs that work and for which hardware and compilers exist have never been transported to other systems.[10] Given that Java has been given an international standard, there is no reason to think that Java programs will drift into uselessness any time soon, especially since many browsers are designed to interpret Java programs in particular. Nonetheless, the McGraw and Tew system does facilitate fairly extensive multimedia reliant research; it is intended to be freely available; and it is designed around the premise that Internet-mediated research creates access to unfathomable numbers of participants.

For the remainder of this section we focus on systems akin to that of McGraw and Tew (1997) that are intended as venues for researchers to create materials and manage research data without knowing the intricacies of Java or other higher-level programming languages (such as the Authorware tools). One system is that of Kenny (1998) and the other is that under development in the Computational Linguistics Lab, at Trinity College, University of Dublin (Guennouni, 2000; Kenny, 1998; McGowan, 1999; Timothy 2000). The former is intended for a user to obtain as a complete system, rather than as a multiple-experiment host site, although multiple conditions are supported. It is further constrained by implementation with certain paradigms of psycholinguistics studies in mind. In particular, it is designed for sentence-completion and magnitude-estimation tasks; however, these study structures have obvious application in other domains. The system offers a stylised language for the user to create instructions to the system for organising experimental materials, for example randomised presentation (modulo constraints that the user may stipulate) of materials, monitoring of response times, and generation of offline questionnaires. The system is implemented in Java under the UNIX operating system, so a researcher with an Internet-accessible UNIX machine can construct studies and present them over the Web, confident that Java-enabled browsers can access them.

There are some useful and clever features in this system. Among them are techniques adopted for participant authentification. For example, the participant is required to provide an email address as part of the accessing process. At the end of a study, an email is sent to the participant. The value of this to the researcher is that if the email bounces back, the researcher has information that the participant might be bogus. Additional security is built in verifying that addresses are used only one time (clearly not desirable for longitudinal studies, but extremely valuable to other studies).[11] A range of useful features are provided by this system, which is distributed free of charge for non-commercial purposes (subject to a licence agreement). Additionally, a mailing list (*webexp@ cogsci.ed.ac.uk*) is associated with ongoing developments to the system. The only faults of the system are limits to the experimental materials and the assumptions it makes about UNIX programming proficiency of the users, even though it does eliminate the need for the researcher to embark on Java programming.

The Dublin system is more like that of McGraw and Tew (1997) in providing a way for the researcher to be completely separated from programming concerns. However, its fault is that it is not yet released (although it has been put to use in three preliminary stages: McGowan, 1999; Ryan, 2001; Timothy, 2000). The currently available features of this system are: researcher design and update of experimental materials consisting of dynamically created web pages; randomised presentation of designated pages; randomisation of stimuli presented on pages; multiple-choice question specification (with optional randomisation of answer choices during presentation); open-ended answers; pre-test and post-test instructions and commentary; and monitoring of page access onset, page offset, and page-internal event times (button clicks, and so on). (The system of Keller et al. [1998] also manages this sort of response-time monitoring, with similar caveats to those expressed here.) Features intended but not yet fully implemented are researcher account management (which will thereby enable a facility like that of McGraw and Tew [1997] that allows multiple researchers to create and manage their studies remotely from the Dublin host), automated extraction of data into formats compatible with statistical analysis packages, participant authentification security measures, and inclusion of graphics in materials by naming an URL at study-creation time.

The system is implemented in Java in a UNIX environment, and it presents the researcher with webpages over the Internet through which he or she can interact with the system, filling in blanks in forms to supply materials, and answering questions about how they should appear on a slide and how they should be presented, while knowing virtually nothing about the underlying programming language. Like the McGraw and Tew (1997) system, it offers the researcher space on a remote host for his or her study, data, and logs. The system is based on the Apache web server, which yields for free a number of the intended features (and which have therefore been neglected as they pose less interesting problems to incorporate), such as researcher/participant account security. We have not yet explored participant authentification techniques to the extent that Keller et al. (1998) have. However, as an ongoing project, the system offers considerable promise to the researcher who desires a secure environment for constructing studies and having data maintained. Certainly, the pilot studies conducted using the preliminary version of the system have benefited from its flexibility.

In sum, the technology for running advanced multimedia studies interactively over the Internet is still under development. While a great number of products exist for purchase or for free, a number of them come with inherent limitations either in excessive demands on the technological prowess of the researcher or the participant (or both) or with constraints on the level of equipment a study (or participant) must have easy access to in order to become involved. Nonetheless, not every study requires sounds, graphics, or animations. A great many can be facilitated by modest FTP transfers or email communication, particularly if the research is based on questionnaires. These techniques create more responsibility for the researcher in maintaining control over the data (for example, ensuring that distinct conditions are inaccessible to participants, who should not be able to download them, and with methods of verifying this control). Nor are they immune to difficulties. In an FTP setting the researcher must decide whether to allow both upload and download of files. Few systems administrators who control researchers' computing facilities allow anonymous uploading, and certainly researchers would be at risk of losing important data in a setting in which participants are allowed to log in and anonymously deposit data, possibly destructively, on top of previously uploaded files. A more secure alternative requires the researcher to obtain individual accounts with permissions for each participant to write files. However, in times of increased monitoring of network security, many network systems administrators are also reluctant to grant such privileges to outside users.

Generally, the FTP setting is best suited to participants downloading materials and responding to them in some form of email reply. This at least abets cross-checking of access logs and email timestamps (though accuracy cannot be guaranteed in the latter case), as well as information about the remote host that forms part of the logs in both, and that can be used for authentification.[12] Just as interactive models of research can be sensitive to network-lag time, so too can FTP. User connections can timeout after seriously long delays. This tends to have an impact on large file transfers (just as the multimedia interactions involve enormous amounts of data movement), but there are also issues with having users transfer a large number of small files: it becomes very easy for a remote user to overlook one or more. While it is possible to create tar files (or the equivalent) that bundle things together, this can make the single data transfer too large in some cases, but worse, more explicit instructions are required for participants who are not familiar with how to unbundle the files. In very few words, the researcher is best advised to keep instrumentation requirements at the minimum acceptable to the research question. We have noticed in our collaborations that ordinary email communications with colleagues in certain geopolitical regions need to be as 'light' as possible for reasons of local economy.[13] In such situations, fully interactive multimedia is not an option and therefore excludes most potential participants. However, provided the researcher adopts a sensible sampling technique, appropriate to the research domain (inclusive of appropriately screening respondents), the Internet can provide a very cheap mode of access to appropriately equipped participants in research.

Methodology

Because of the ease of access to participants in Internet-based research, it is somehow equally easy to make silly methodological mistakes, some more or less devastating than others. One of the issues discussed at length in Chapter 3 was identifying the appropriate sampling strategy. It may be desirable to send an email that invites replies to express interest in participating to a large number of Web forums, Internet lists, chat rooms, and so on, where these are selected more or less on the basis of size of accessed community and focal point of the community interest. However, at the extreme of such participation solicitation, it is important to ensure that all the announcements are correct in all details, and that the full study is sorted out: once one has made one wide-fan solicitation, it is methodologically suspect to make a second call for a minor variant of the study. Of course, this is no different than in research situations away from the Internet. However, the relative ease of hitting the 'Send' button on an incomplete message or providing undesirable access to materials and conditions, in comparison with more traditional methods for spoiling one's participant pool, is as mind-boggling as the extreme scale of the pool of potential participants afforded by the Internet. It has never been so easy to so quickly invalidate the participation of so many participants. This issue is paramount in constructing studies to be administered via the Internet.

Most other methodological issues are the same in the case of Internet-mediated research as in other modes of research. All of the traditional issues must be sorted out before actually soliciting any participants, and that may create certain timetabling issues: Internet traffic is far greater during the academic year than outside it; Internet traffic troughs during holiday periods widely internationally celebrated. Any study with a critical amount of time between conditions should be sensitive to both global fluctuations and constancies in the availability of participants. This simply means that there are more methodological issues to consider, and that the traditional ones (including the correct way of soliciting and screening participants for the task at hand) need to be sorted out early on. Chapter 3 raised the ethical dimensions of this issue.

At least one other methodological issue is more or less unique to studies administered via the Internet, and is particularly important to studies involving participants in collaborative dialogue (Healey, 1995). Relevant case studies will be outlined in Chapter 7. The basic issue at stake is the potential difference between synchronous and asynchronous communication made possible by the Internet. Previously we have emphasised the advantages offered by asynchronous communication, notably (say, in comparison to a questionnaire administered by telephone) that the participant can respond at greater leisure (Hewson et al.,

1996). For those studies in which the completion time of materials is irrelevant, that can be an advantage in obtaining more thoughtful and cooperative responses. However, the Internet also offers access to approximately synchronous and fully synchronous communications. Email is again an example of the former category, and IRC, chat rooms, MOOs, and so on are examples of the latter. Whether at adjacent machines in the same lab or accessing machines from opposite sides of the globe, it is possible to use email in a nearly synchronous fashion.[14] The methodological upshot of this is that it can become important to a study to know the geographical location of the participants. Traditional collaborative dialogue studies involve participants situated locally, and the issue of time-zone differences does not arise. However, it is a potentially important fact to know whether one's participants are participating in the wee hours of the morning or during what ought to have been lunchtime, by their local watch. A corollary is that it can be difficult to timetable specific joint cooperation for nearly synchronous events between participants who have never met; it is far from impossible, but it remains an additional methodological issue for the researcher to resolve. The issue is that potential fatigue of participants usually does not have to be monitored in (nearly) synchronous tasks locally executed, but it nearly certainly does have to be monitored in the case of Internet-mediated research because of the vast geographical distances that may be involved. While video-conferencing and telephone interviews are accompanied by the same constraints, the former is as new as IMR (and in many cases actually is administered via the Internet), and the latter simply is not practical.

A host of methodological issues need to be settled because the Internet administration of a study raises a whole host of methodological issues needing to be settled that would not occur in other settings, but this need not be problematic, depending on the research question. One that has been discussed is how the researcher and user accounts are named – anonymously or not, with gendered names, or not, and so on. Another is in informing participants that all of their communications will be recorded (but rendered anonymous in reporting situations). Just as it becomes relevant to many linguistic judgement tasks to know facts about an individual's handedness (Schütze, 1996), when studies are administered via the Internet and involve rapid production of texts by the participants (perhaps in a communicative setting), then it becomes relevant to have a preliminary screening that allows balancing for typing prowess.[15] Further, depending on how remote reaction-time studies are arranged, it is also necessary to know the handedness of the participants as well as the degree to which their hardware setup, in conjunction with the experimental interface with which they are confronted, is attuned to their handedness requirements. For example, the location of the 'yes' and 'no' – accept and reject keys – on a keyboard could correspond to the alphabetic 'y' and 'n' keys, which, on the standard keyboard, are not optimally positioned for balanced ease of depression, or could map to two other keys that have significantly different positioning, or to buttons on a mouse.

A similar issue to control for (or at least to obtain questionnaire data about) is whether the participant has free email access from home (or workplace) and whether emails sent from the workplace are monitored. It is sometimes important to know whether the respondent is participating from home or workplace as well. Of course, the factor at stake is the degree of leisure and freedom that the participant feels. However, the range of questioning is obviously delicate, as some respondents-from-work might easily be put off, suspecting the study itself as a form of management monitoring. A connected issue is that it is important to offer a participant opportunities to withdraw from the study (without crashing the server that runs the study). This issue was developed further in Chapter 3; the methodological/ethical issues relevant here are guarantees of anonymity of even partial participation, and whether partial data is to be analysed at all or deleted wholesale. On the other hand, in many work settings daytime diversions are encouraged. In any case, it is valuable to know the actual constraints the participant is operating under. Knowing that the participant pays for email separate from Internet access can provide an independent explanation for brevity of reply in some cases. Equally, free Internet access can inspire a different length of participation in studies not based on email but still relying on Internet interactions. Thus, we advocate including questions that solicit information on that range of issues in any pre-study exercise that screens participants.

Finally, other sociological effects may have to be controlled for in some studies: there is unprecedented capacity for individuals to misrepresent themselves and their personality traits in Internet interactions, to the extent of adopting alternative personae for their Internet interactions from their 'real-life' interactions. Certainly, aggressive behaviours can be manifest in Internet communications in ways that are not apparent in other forms of social interaction. These facts about communicative styles are an important topic of current research and must be addressed in any study that hopes to generalize from Internet-based communication styles to communication in general (Berzsenyi, 1999; Herring, 1996; Kiesler et al., 1984; Rossetti, 1998).

Netiquette

Solicitation of participants is one part of the research phase that interacts with 'netiquette' (see Chapter 2). This is particularly relevant to USE-NEWS newsgroups and email lists, which have developed a certain canon of acceptable behaviours, some of which Internet researchers can easily infringe. One of the basic rules is that postings (to either) should 'be relevant'. This in particular can run counter to the needs of many studies in which one explicitly does not want to post invitations to participate in a study on a particular topic to a group or list devoted to discussion of that topic (of course, this is not always the case). Note that it is possible to select target locations at random within any mode of Internet access (lists, newsgroups, and so on), provided one has an enumeration of them to select at random from (or to select on the basis of discussion content). However, as pointed out in Chapter 4, it is important to keep in mind that not all locations yield access to the same numbers of potential participants. Thus, if one is balancing solicitations across locations defined by contrasting topics of discussion, one is not necessarily balancing solicitations across even population sizes. This can be controlled for somewhat by monitoring degree of activity in the relevant locations.

One's invitation to participate in the study is nearly always completely irrelevant to the main intended discussion. And in this case one is hopeful for the generosity of moderators (in cases where moderation exists) to not disallow the posting. In many cases, by approaching moderators directly initially, this particular constraint can be overcome. However, it is crucial not to be deemed as posting profiteering 'spam'. One thing to pay particular attention to is that there are also Net vigilantes who do not directly moderate lists, but who have an apparently syntactic definition of what constitutes 'spam'. Hewson and Vogel (1994), for example, found their invitations cancelled when they were posted to more than 20 newsgroups at a time, regardless of whether there was a semantically uniting relationship among the groups or a purely scientific non-commercial motive to the ad: posting to more than 20 newsgroups at a time is what certain Net vigilantes deem to be unacceptable, and can result in having to repost in smaller numbers. Therefore, it is important never to exceed that threshold.[16] While it is tempting to suggest the alternative response, to post to each individually, this also violates the netiquette of 'crossposting': in order to save bandwidth it is desirable to have one copy of the text around rather than multiple copies, one in each group. There is a difference in how many times an individual participant will see the notice. (This is a salient difference between newsgroups and mailing lists, in fact. For mailing lists even crossposting to multiple lists entails that a multiply subscribed individual will run across the ad in each setting, while an ad crossposted to newsgroups will be seen by a reader only in the first group the reader is subscribed to where it is encountered.)

One final point is that ads posted to email lists and newsgroups should be formulated in text-only format so that they can be read on any news or mail reader;[17] in particular, they should not be posted as attachments nor include attachments. It has become quite easy for PC users to send computer viruses to other users without even realising that their own computers are infected. Sending viruses will alienate a great many participants, and if they focus on a virus itself, particularly because of the fairly random contact made between researcher and participant, a researcher could easily find the ad circulating the globe with cautions to avoid reading messages about the study as it is 'false and contains simply a virus'.[18]

The researcher using attachments can fairly quickly become (and render all Internet researchers) a global pariah. The best way to avoid the problem is to refrain from using attachments altogether and to stick to text-based messaging.[19] At least two less invasive alternative methods exist for obtaining participants. One is to use the experiment clearing-house approach mentioned earlier. In this method, the researcher designs a study to be located in a place in which a number of other studies are hosted. These tend to become familiar to the community of teachers in the human sciences who will have their students participate in studies that are created on the Web, and thus have a more or less cyclical flow of participants coursing through them. In addition to the educational community, one might also have interested lay parties, such as avid crossword solvers, seeking out such things to participate in. However, these latter participants come with self-selection characteristics that may not be desirable for a study depending on a wide sample of the population. The student population may also be skewed for some purposes. Another possibility is to take advantage of free web-page hosting and the mechanics of Internet search engines. Some Internet companies earn their living by obtaining high 'hit rates' for web pages. The adaptation of their essential trick is to place a modest web page on a separate site from the study, but with a host of tagwords attached to the page. The choice of tagwords can be tailored to the sort of domain subject interest one is hoping to obtain participants from. For example, in a study about attitudes towards immigration, one could encode into the free page as many of the words associated with the topic as possible. Thus, the free page, along with a link to the study, has a greater chance of being identified during a random potential participant's search of the Internet for information about the topic.

Equally, one can load the keywords with a completely random set of tags, or one can employ only very frequently searched tags if one wants to obtain the widest pool possible.[20] Using this method, one can attract participants without cluttering their favourite newsgroup or their mailbox with postings. A related technique is to place pointers to the study on domain-connected (or -unconnected) chat pages. These are DHTML pages that accept small texts from users and leave them posted for subsequent readers. They are unlike newsgroups in that postings do not expire nearly as rapidly. (This can have its own annoyances once a study has ended, so this last form of participant gathering should be approached cautiously.) In fact, in virtually any of the currently available forums for individuals to communicate synchronously or asynchronously over the Internet (see Chapter 2), it is possible to advertise for participants in a study. The suitability of each method depends on the factors discussed above: the longevity of the notice, the suitability of the participant pool accessed, and the size of the pool. The differences are in that in varying settings it can be more or less difficult to advertise.

Hackers

It is an odd thing about the Internet that one can easily have a substantial number of people actively looking for studies to participate in. One can equally have a substantial number of people searching the Web looking for ways to test their skills in cracking into systems and having an impact on them. In connection with Internet-mediated research, some of these individuals will appear in the guise of participants, and some of them will simply be attempting to break into the site, with little interest in the study that is running. Password-cracking programs abound freely on the Net, and a typical exercise for novice hackers is to attempt to obtain illicit access to a system by breaking into accounts. There are standard safeguards against this practice, and they come with varying degrees of hassle for the researcher. The first issue is with user account names for participants allowed system privileges on the researcher's host system. In general, a hacker requires both a user ID and a password to gain access. Therefore, one can protect oneself to some extent by not positing a very predictable set of user IDs. However, once a potential intruder identifies an actual user ID for the account, it becomes possible to test out arbitrarily many possible passwords.

Consequently, it is very important that a sensible strategy for generating passwords be identified. Systems administrators are the best source of tips on this, but in short the passwords should not be words or names found in dictionaries for any human language; they should contain combinations of uppercase and lowercase letters, as well as numeric characters.[21] The effects of random hackers intent on breaking into accounts can usually be forestalled that way. However, if they do gain access, then it is important to identify this and close the leak as soon as possible. Again, systems administrators have standard ways of monitoring this – generally this involves monitoring access logs to verify that access is made to the systems from known remote hosts, and to verify that datafiles do not suddenly disappear or radically change in properties (such as size). System backups may provide partial recovery from the effects of hackers.

Researchers should ensure, whether through an experiment clearing-house facility or on the researcher's own hosting site, that all materials associated with the study and data obtained from it are located in places that are not permitted to external readers without clearance. That is, web pages are usually accessed through a specific URL (for example, *www.york.ac.uk/inst/ctipsych/expgen/ entry.html*); however, unless permissions are set appropriately, it is also possible for anyone at all to view files listed at higher points in the directory structure. For example, at the time of writing, anyone in the world with a web browser can examine the URL related to the one just mentioned in passing above – to find the information shown in Table 6.1.

In the case of access via a web browser, this effect is avoided by placing an index.html file in each directory (and controlling permissions on files and directories). With such a file in place, its contents will be viewed and processed by the client browser, but not the accompanying information about directory structure, file names, file sizes, date of update, and so on. Of course, the extent to which this matters depends entirely on the intended security of the files that are made visible in this way.

In this case the files available are not alternative conditions in a study. Certainly, in most circumstances involving separate conditions in a study, one does not want the alternative conditions to be visible to participants. Moreover, ethical considerations interact here (see Chapter 3). In most cases, one does not want to make prior participant data freely visible to new participants, or to anyone for that matter. The extent to which visibility of files to random hackers can result in data loss or other disruptions of a study is less clear, but caution (certainly regarding confidentially) suggests that most materials and directory structures and file-naming schemes should be quite invisible to everyone.

The primary other issue associated with hacking behaviour is the participation of participants who are keen to discover things about

Table 6.1   *Index of /inst/ctipsych/expgen*

Name	Last modified	Size	Description
Parent Directory	21-Mar-2001 13.49	–	
PEL-add.html	11-Dec-1998 13.49	2k	CTI Directory of Psych >
PEL-intro.html	11-Dec-1998 13:49	3k	CTI Directory of Psych >
PEL-sub-txt.html	11-Dec-1998 14:43	7k	CTI Directory pf Psych >
PEL-submit.html	11-Dec-1998 14:40	8k	CTI Directory pf Psych >
Psyscope/	01-Dec-1997 14:14	–	
entry.html	11-Dec-1998 13:49	9k	CTI Directory pf Psych >
subs.ltd/	10-Dec-1998 16:22	–	
wishform.html	12-Jul-1999 11:26	3k	CTI Directory pf Psych >
wishmenu.html	12-Jul-1999 11:30	3k	CTI Directory pf Psych >
wishreply.html	11-Dec-1998 13:49	4k	CTI Directory pf Psych >

Source: *www.york.ac.uk/inst/ctipsych/expgen/*

the study prematurely[22] or who are simply bent on derailing the results. Ways that an individual might do this is by multiple participation or attempting to examine other conditions. We have just discussed how file permissions should be set to prevent the possibility of participants consciously wandering into other experimental conditions. However, it is also important to give semantically unrelated names (and not minimal alphabetic variants) to directories for various conditions, or to files for distinct conditions within the same directory. The reason for this is that even without a hacker mentality, a participant could easily wander via typographical error or free association from the provided URL into a URL for a distinct condition. Similarly, an individual might attempt to participate in a study (say, a survey) more than once. Protections against this hinge on monitoring the domain address from which a user accesses the study. This, of course, is not a completely ideal method since there can be more than one user for an individual machine, and more than one user may participate in any given study.[23] The technique of Keller et al. (1998) to identify whether participants are bogus can be applied here as well to a limited extent. They demanded that participants supply email addresses (which can, but do not necessarily, incorporate the domain address of the host to which they connect from: for example, a user may have an account on one machine, but handle all email from a remote host, such as via a Yahoo.com account). At the end of the study a 'thank you' email is sent to the participant, and if it bounces back there is a fair chance that the participant is bogus. The technique can equally be used to monitor for multiple participation. When a single domain address (or closely related one) turns up in the log files for more than one user, it can be verified whether the same or different email address was associated with each login. Of course, it is possible for a hacker to have more than one email address, but the possibility of a hacker having a sufficient number of distinct addresses to derail the study diminishes rapidly. Consider the problems faced by the online auction industry as an example of the reality of the problem in non-research domains. Dobrzynski (2000) reports on the monitoring practices of eBay, the Internet auction agency, to prevent individuals with multiple addresses (or actual cartels) from bidding up their own offerings. A difficult problem in this monitoring process is exactly that users can have more than one login, and can enter the system from more than one host. Thus, this is not a guaranteed safeguard, and guarantees of single participation remain a topic of research.

It is also a good idea to rely on software that provides assurance of testing under adverse conditions (whether second-hand software or researcher-produced interactive web pages). Here a significant issue is with the standard use of cut-and-paste familiar from word-processing packages. It is easy to overlook having highlighted enormous amounts of text (and as easy intentionally to highlight the same) and with the click of a key dump the entire wad into a text box in some form or other. Now this is not necessarily problematic; however, if the pasted text includes various control codes (such as explicit HTML encoding), many systems can suffer consequent data loss. The reason is that field delimiters in the underlying database are suddenly used within one field. The result is a software confusion about where the field boundaries are, and corruption of data from that point on. Similarly, if an encoded URL is included in a text box, perhaps in an online communication task, one can suddenly find that another participant has clicked on the URL and find the browser launched to some site external to the study.[24] The way to guard against these problems is to test software rigorously in advance with unintended inputs (such as null inputs, garbage inputs, random HTML, large files, and so on).

Again, with the ease with which IMR brings a study quickly online comes a commensurate responsibility to avoid doing so too soon, and before appropriate piloting. This is related to a point raised in Chapter 3 on the topic of ethics: it is very easy to forward or simply send the data contributed by a participant in confidence to unintended recipients. One must reflect on the ramifications of pressing the equivalent of the 'Send' button at every instance. The results of acting too quickly can be disastrous. There is a direct relationship between pre-study adversarial testing of electronic materials and diminished risk of all sorts at study time.

Summary

In this chapter we have examined four main categories of problems that can arise for studies conducted over the Internet. The first of them is related to equipment available for conducting such studies. We pointed out that the more complex the equipment required, the more limited the pool of potential participants becomes, and the more difficult it is for a non-specialist in programming issues to construct the study. We also provided pointers to a range of studies available on the Internet that currently actively gather data and provide examples of the range of options possible. Discussion of the range of facilities currently or soon to be available to researchers interested in presenting studies on the Internet but disinterested in becoming expert programmers will, it is hoped, provide guidelines to researchers intending to use the Internet. Methodological issues particular to the Internet as well as those common in other areas but exacerbated (or ameliorated) by Internet research were also outlined. The primary issue there is to proceed cautiously and carefully before implementing a study over the Internet, resisting the unprecedented speed of access to participants that it offers. Additionally we suggested guidelines for attracting participants, and provided pointers

on how to avoid problems that arise from attracting recalcitrant participants and outright hackers.

Notes

1   In this chapter we focus on IMR using primary research means – studies of various
    sorts that rely on the Internet for access to participants. Chapter 2 discussed methodo-
    logical issues with secondary research (as distinguished in Chapter 1) in which the
    Internet is used as a point of access to information codifying primary research. The
    primary methodological risks discussed in Chapter 2 were: too much trust in a
    particular Internet resource, and habituation to the idea that Internet resources are the
    only ones worth checking.
2   Text-based systems like Lynx have also been addressed in this book, but for the
    moment we will focus on the multimedia-enabled sorts.
3   However, Chapter 5 provides a primer.
4   Chapter 4 also points out ways that systems can have unexpected behaviours.
5   This point will be resumed later, and in additional contexts (see also Chapter 4).
6   Chapter 4 points to the issue of Internet use by vision-impaired individuals. Some
    users in this population do have speech synthesis facilities, as pointed out in Chapter
    4. The methodologically relevant point here is to encourage HTML encoding that
    maximises use of meta-tags identifying materials so that visually impaired participants
    can know what they are not seeing, and to include questioning about whether a
    participant relies on such facilitating access software in any study for which it is a
    critical issue. See also *www.rnib.org.uk/wedo/research/access.htm* for tips on making web
    pages accessible to vision-impaired individuals.
7   Chapter 4 pointed out as well that for some studies in which only one browser may
    offer the requisite behaviour for the stimulus materials, it may be necessary simply to
    restrict participation to individuals with the appropriate browser. Of course, this
    applies to equipment generally.
8   See also discussion of 'cookies' in Chapter 4.
9   Note that many studies currently exist on the Web, and one can easily stumble upon
    them. We suspect that for many purposes, these studies are not controlled enough for
    participant access. Some example clearing houses of studies implemented to obtain
    participants via the Web are as follows:

    - *coglab.wadsworth.com*
    - *www.apa.org/monitor/aprodresearch.box2.html*
    - *kahuna.psych.uiuc.edu/ipl/*
    - *www.cops.uni-sb.de/ronald/ONLINE/online_e.htm*
    - *www-mugc.cc.monash.edu.au/psy/ol/www_lab.html*
    - *www.psych.unizh.ch/genpsy/Ulf/Lab/WebExpPsyLab.html*
    - *www.york.ac.uk/inst/ctipsych/expgen/entry.html*

    However, a problem akin to the one faced by researchers whose participants change
    their home Internet access during the course of a study is that of Internet resources
    becoming accessed by alternative URL names, or dropping out of existence altogether.
    Note as well that not all of the studies available above are intended for Internet
    participation. Some are designed for downloading over the Internet and execution on
    local hosts; others are designed for experiment generation, but not necessarily studies
    that run in an Internet-accessible mode, and certainly not necessarily cheaply available
    (in particular see *www.york.ac.uk/inst/ctipsych/expgen/entry.html*).

10 Worries about some of these programs were fundamental to the Y2K hysteria, and it remains possible to sustain oneself by maintaining programs written in unfashionable languages like COBOL and FORTRAN.

11 See Chapter 4 for elaboration of the problem of identifying individual participants by host identification status, or even user ID. The latter case offers the most insidious risks as it becomes impossible to verify the actual identity of participants, and thus even the true number of participants. If one has participants in a study whose access is defined in this way, then in some cases it is better if there is a single (trusted) coordinator for the user ID who can attest to the authenticity of each participant's contributions. On the other hand, for some research questions, this model compromises the candidness of participants: they may feel doubly observed.

12 Modulo issues were raised earlier in this chapter and in Chapter 4 with regard to participant authentification versus host/user ID identification.

13 Additionally, there can be difficulties that emerge due to the impoverished nature of ASCII character encoding for languages that make extensive use of diacritics. Character-set encoding incompatibilities can also cause technical problems in transfer of materials. Appel and Mullen (2000) also offer reflections on this issue.

14 Here, increased network traffic means slower communication at the same time that it entails a potentially larger participant pool; however, the resulting implications for level of equipment possessed by both researcher and participant becomes prohibitive.

15 In multimedia settings, this can be avoided by using speech-to-speech communications, much like a telephone; however, the resulting implications for level of equipment possessed by both researcher and participant becomes prohibitive.

16 Our experience was that rational discussion was of no use, it was utterly irrelevant that we were not sending chain letters or seeking profits; simply exceeding the 20-address rule caused us considerable wastage of time.

17 In general, to assure the widest possible audience (as mentioned earlier), it is also desirable to constrain the study itself in this way. However, Chapter 4 points out that certain studies may require parochial hardware and software constraints.

18 This stands in spite of the point made in Chapter 2 that most virus warnings have been bogus. The effect of association with a bogus, yet globally circulated, virus warning is immeasurable.

19 As an aside here, the researcher should probably also consider creating a distinct user account for each study embarked upon. This is not the same as using a distinct return email address for each, with all responses directed towards one basic account. Having separate accounts, without consolidated mail forwarding, enables the researcher to keep correspondence about multiple studies distinct and by localizing them in individual accounts. It is possible to set many mailers to file incoming messages automatically on the basis of subject line or recipient, but potential participants do not always maintain the same subject line as the original posting, so that the method of filing incoming mail is not completely effective. Additionally, many actual spam producers trawl the Internet looking for email addresses to send things to. Keeping separate accounts for separate studies therefore has the advantage of avoiding a lot of junk mail in the researcher's personal email account. This is also a useful protection against the occasional participant who becomes obsessed with continued correspondence with the researcher – the researcher can after a time simply stop checking on updated correspondence to a particular account when its usefulness has expired.

20 This method is interestingly different from the technique that results in sending a USENEWS posting to *rec.pets.aardvark*, discussed in Chapter 4. Here, hits arise because for whatever reason a prospective participant has sought out the relevant tag.

21 Reporting this here does not compromise the efficacy of the strategy: the password-cracking programs have to check all possible combinations of case and numerics. Typical systems administrators monitor and prevent repeated login attempts that

continue for extended periods. Of course, occasionally monitoring slips, and the researcher should be as aware of the illicit login monitoring facilities at the home site as of the file backup frequency.

22 We acknowledge the value of disclosure during debriefing, however (see Chapter 3).

23 Problems in monitoring this were discussed earlier in this chapter, as well as in Chapter 4.

24 In some studies it is important to know whether participants have consulted external data sources. Additionally, it is a common bug in nascent Internet experiment management systems for transfer to external hosts to freeze the server, effectively crashing it. It is certainly a common enough bug that one should try it out during pilots using a system.

7

Case Studies

Here we present three case studies intended to give examples of the various ways in which Internet-mediated research can be implemented, and to outline the problems that were encountered and ways in which these were overcome. The studies were carried out by ourselves and our colleagues between 1994 and 2000. The first case study provides an example of a simple email-based methodology, whereby participants were contacted via newsgroups, and sent an experimental text-based questionnaire by email. The second case study describes a Web-based experiment, involving a more complex procedure, and requiring software that is able to generate a series of stimuli from a table of conditional probabilities, invoke random presentation of trials, and send data back to the web server after each trial. Various obstacles occurred in developing this experiment, and these are highlighted along with description of solutions and subsequent improvements. The final case study describes some research into second-language acquisition that used the Internet to access participants. A system was developed that allowed for the collection of transcripts of interactions between participants who were taking part in 'tandem language learning'. The system developed is described in terms of how it was able to enhance levels of researcher control and incorporate other useful features. Lessons to be learned from these examples are summarised.

Case Study 1: Empirical Evidence Regarding the Folk Psychological Concept of Belief

C. Hewson

An early attempt to make use of the Internet as a data-gathering tool involved a study I carried out in 1994 (Hewson, 1994) that set out to examine the commonsense concept of belief. The purpose of the study was to test some claims made within the folk psychology debate about the nature of our everyday commonsense (folk psychological) notion of belief (Double, 1985; Stich, 1983). The procedure adopted was very simple and made use of USENET to advertise the study, and email to administer materials and collect data. What follows is a description of this procedure, followed by some reflections on issues arising and possible improvements. This case study provides a good example of how the Internet may be used for data gathering, without the need for sophisticated technological implementations.

Procedure

The experimental procedure presented participants with two short stories, each followed by a question. Participants were simply required to read each story and answer the question. Details of the experimental manipulations can be found in Hewson (1994) but are not necessary here. Essentially, eight distinct questionnaires were constructed for distribution to participants.

Initially participants were recruited by approaching seminar tutors and asking permission to administer materials during a seminar session. This resulted in a sample of 15 undergraduate psychology students. However, since this method did not elicit many responses, and proved time-consuming, it was decided that an Internet-mediated approach might prove beneficial in obtaining further data more time-effectively. To this end a participation request was sent to a selection of USENET newsgroups, for example *cogsci.general* and *eduni.general*. Other newsgroups targeted were psychology-related. The request was brief and to the point, simply stating that participants were required to take part in a study on people's commonsense understanding of beliefs. Interested parties were asked to contact the researcher by email. Within two weeks of posting this request, 135 responses had been obtained.[1]

The non-Internet sample was handed the questionnaires to complete during a seminar session, with the researcher (and seminar tutor) present. The Internet sample was sent the questionnaires via email. Since materials comprised of plain text it was easy simply to paste the appropriate file into the body of an email message. The version of the questionnaire sent was determined by participant response sequence, so that the first respondent received questionnaire 1, the second respondent questionnaire 2, and so on (the non-Internet sample was also given versions in rotation). A record was kept of the version sent to each participant by creating a log of participants' email addresses and an indication of which questionnaire had been sent to that address. Instructions to participants were conveyed in a sentence, immediately prior to the story, which asked them simply to read the story, answer the question that followed, and send their response back to the researcher by email. The questionnaires also asked for details of participants' educational background as it was considered that this factor might influence responses.

As participants sent their responses back, these were saved, each to a unique file (in a subdirectory on the researcher's university account). The log of email addresses alongside materials administered turned out to be useful at this stage since a number of participants sent back answers without the original materials appended. Thus the record allowed tracing of the version of the questionnaire that had been sent to these individuals. As responses were received, an email was sent back that thanked participants for taking part, briefly explained the nature of the study, and offered further information upon request. In order to run analysis on the data, it was necessary to categorise responses to each question as 'yes', 'no', or 'ambiguous'. These responses were stored in another datafile in an appropriate format for analysis using BMDP software (log linear analysis was used).[2] Participants' additional comments and explanations were also noted.

Discussion

The Internet-mediated procedure was highly successful in generating a large sample of participants in a short space of time and with minimal costs. Participation postings were only sent to a handful of newsgroups, yet in only two weeks 135 responses were received.[3] Photocopying costs were reduced by sending materials in electronic format. Demands on the researcher's time were reduced since materials could be sent to multiple participants, and incoming data saved, in a matter of minutes. Compare this with the time involved in arranging to attend a seminar session, photocopying materials, describing the procedure to participants, and waiting for them to complete the questionnaire. It was also clear that the Internet sample was more diverse than the non-Internet sample, at least in terms of age and occupation. Many of the Internet sample provided very elaborate and detailed explanations for their responses, which proved useful in the data analysis phase. This contrasted with the non-Internet sample, though this difference could be accountable to either the nature of the different procedures used, or differences in the samples themselves.

However, problems did arise. One unforeseen problem concerned a moderator from one of the newsgroups objecting to the call for participation posting. This moderator contacted the researcher with a harsh email stating that the posting was unauthorised, unsuitable, and had been removed. An apology was sent in reply and that was the end of the issue. While the other postings did not provoke such a reaction, it is, in retrospect, always advisable to contact the moderator of a newsgroup before posting any call for participation.[4] If the study is presented as genuine, well-motivated, and affiliated with a recognised organisation then there should rarely be a problem. Nevertheless, authorisation should always be sought in advance where possible.

A further problem that was not predicted was that a small number of respondents actually sent their replies from different email accounts to their original response. Thus the tracking procedure that identified participants by email addresses failed in these cases. Fortunately these respondents made the situation explicit to the researcher. However, this highlights the ineffectiveness of the tracking procedure employed here to deal with such situations. An alternative may be to assign participants a password and ask them to quote this when they return their data. Tracking participants is a general problem in IMR, and more research into the most effective procedures is needed (see, especially, Chapter 4 for discussion of this issue). A further point already mentioned is worth re-emphasising: some participants returned their responses without including the original materials sent. As it happens, the tracking procedure employed made this unproblematic in this case. However, this possibility was not anticipated. This highlights the importance of making instructions clear and explicit, and not presuming that participants will behave in a certain way. Taking care to make sure that all information that may be important to the study is recorded is thus important, though not always possible to anticipate. Piloting of any study is highly recommended since there is always room for possibilities that the researcher does not foresee.

Suggestions for Improvement

The sampling methodology employed here could have been more carefully considered. The newsgroups targeted were selected because they were familiar (to the researcher), but in hindsight this sampling procedure was bound to reach a fairly select group of individuals; in particular those working in academia, and with a particular interest in psychology. Given the nature of the research topic a less specialist sample would probably have been preferable. It would have been easy to select a larger and broader range of newsgroups to post participation requests to, had this been considered at the time.[5] Nevertheless the decision to collect information about educational experience was useful – a number of respondents reported having had training in cognitive science and/or logic, and, as suspected, this appeared to have an influence on their responses (consequently these responses were omitted in the final analysis). Additional demographic information would also have been useful to further investigate sampling bias.

The expiry date for the call for participation postings was not set (see discussion in Chapter 4). It would have been useful to determine, or at least monitor, the exposure period for postings. Doing so gives the researcher more control over data collection. As it happens, this study received a large number of replies in a short period. If more responses are required, then setting a longer exposure period can be useful. If response rates are still low, then re-postings to the same newsgroups is a possibility, though checking with the newsgroup moderator before re-posting a call is essential in order to avoid any offence or misunderstanding.

While the time- and cost-efficiency of using USENET and email to gather data was noted, the incoming data were printed out in hard copy format. Clearly costs could have been further reduced if this had been avoided. At the time, hard copies were printed out as backup, due to concerns about possible data loss. However, this method is not maximally efficient and does not take advantage of some of the obvious benefits of IMR. It would have been better to create duplicate backup files, and employ methods such as those described in Chapter 6 to ensure data security. This would have avoided incurring additional unnecessary costs.

This study could have implemented ethical guidelines more stringently. While debriefing was carried out in the form of sending an email explaining the study, along with an invitation for further enquiries, no procedure for acquiring informed consent was implemented. At the time it was considered that a response to the postings, expressing a desire to take part in the study, was an adequate indication of consent. However, employing some more formal methodology is advisable (see Chapter 3 for a discussion of how consent may be obtained in IMR). In this particular study, participants could have been asked to 'sign' a consent form by typing in an assigned password, for example.

Conclusions

This case study illustrates well some of the benefits IMR can offer to the researcher who does not have the time and/or expertise to devote to constructing complex designs involving interactive web pages, or other more technically complex procedures. It demonstrates how data can be collected by simply posting participation calls to newsgroups, and using email to administer materials and obtain responses. A limitation of this approach is the lower degree of automation possible, in terms of data collection, coding, and analysis. In a WWW study, submitted data can be sent directly to a file in a form ready for analysis.[6] Further, administration of materials can likewise be automated in a Web-based study. Clearly this can have great benefits in terms of saving time (and costs) during the running of a study. However, this benefit must be weighed up against the time and expertise required to construct such implementations (prior to the study). In some cases, especially those involving smaller sample sizes, or requiring higher levels of researcher–participant interaction, an email approach may still be preferable.

Case Study 2: Decision Making in a Medical Diagnosis Task

P. Yule

In association with colleagues in London, I have been using the Web to present experiments in the cognitive psychology of decision making, with reference to a simple medical diagnosis task derived from that developed by Fox (1980). The task was originally developed in the late 1970s, using a DEC PDP11 computer, driving a VDU, and accepting input from a panel of electrical contacts, which the participant touched with a brass electrode to select among input options. I began constructing an Internet version in 1997, in order to replicate and extend the original findings.

The task itself casts the participant in the role of a doctor, attempting to diagnose a series of patients who present various symptoms, and takes the form of a simple 'conversation'. First, the patient tells the doctor a symptom, selected from a small number (say five) of possibilities: we can imagine the patient complains of vomiting. Then, the doctor can ask about one or more other symptoms, and the patient responds either in the positive or in the negative. Finally, when enough information has been gathered, the participant/doctor makes a diagnosis from one of a small number of possible diseases. Given that the diseases that appear in the experiment are completely fictitious, participants cannot know anything initially, so they must learn by trial and error as the task progresses. The symptom patterns for each disease are actually generated probabilistically from a table of conditional probabilities, and presented in random order across a series of blocks of trials.

The experimental software must be able to generate a series of stimuli (patients) from a table of conditional probabilities, randomise their order, and present the trials individually, recording data for each one and sending it back to a server somehow. The decision was made to write the program as a JavaScript client, so it was convenient to make the client present trials in a series of blocks, randomising each one at the beginning and only sending back the data at the end of each block.

The earliest version of the client did not require a sophisticated server; it was launched by clicking a button at the bottom of a web page of instructions, which opened a new window to present the diagnosis task.

Participants were required to enter a user ID when the client program started, then perform a series of blocks of trials. The user ID was used to identify the data when it was sent back at the end of each block, to be saved using a simple server script like that described in Chapter 5. Given this arrangement, each instance of the client was independent, so it could not be used to administer a between-subjects design.

The interface used for each trial depended on dividing the screen into three sections using frames. A central frame presented the current state of information about the patient, while a pair of frames at the left and right respectively held lists of symptom and disease names. The symptom and disease names were actually implemented as hyperlinks, so that the participant could query a symptom by clicking on its hyperlink in the left frame, or diagnose a disease by clicking on its hyperlink in the right frame. Each link had an associated JavaScript function, which logged the event in a main data array, and caused the information to be displayed incrementally in the centre frame. Figure 7.1 shows a screenshot of the client after two symptoms have been queried.

Unfortunately this arrangement was unsatisfactory, for three reasons. First, it became apparent that the order of the symptom and disease names needed to be randomised, since their fixed onscreen orders were causing query-sequencing artefacts – this was an option which was not

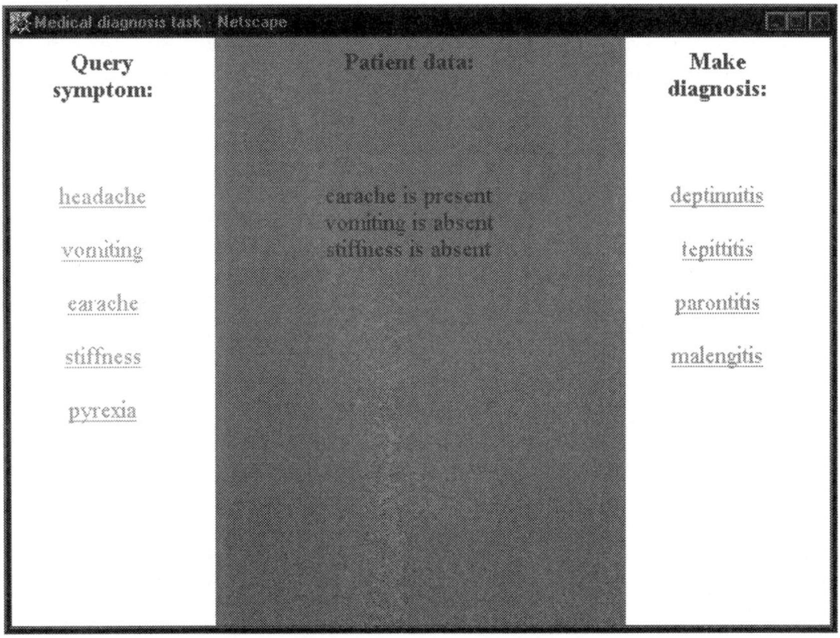

Query symptom:	Patient data:	Make diagnosis:
headache	earache is present	deptinnitis
vomiting	vomiting is absent	tepittitis
earache	stiffness is absent	parontitis
stiffness		malengitis
pyrexia		

Figure 7.1 *Prototype interface for the medical diagnosis task*

open to Fox in his original study. Second, the lack of a sophisticated server made it impossible to perform a desired between-subjects manipulation, which would assign participants to one of two groups and provide different conditional probability tables to each. Finally, writing incrementally to the central frame was not portable between browsers, since it was an operation that was not explicitly supported by the HTML standard; also, when the client window was resized, the information in the central window was lost completely.

Rectifying the first problem of randomisation was fairly easy – it was necessary to make the client generate a different list of symptoms (and diseases) on each trial, so instead of loading a static page into each of the control frames, it was necessary to generate each frame's contents using JavaScript on each trial.

The need to assign participants to one of two groups necessitated development of a server script, which eventually developed into a rather complex system with data tabulation and analysis facilities, facilities for excluding participants' data if required, as well as group allocation and participant-tracking facilities. The main innovation was to start the JavaScript client as the consequence of a CGI request that sent the user ID to the server, allowing the server to provide different versions of the client to the two groups, to whom it allocated participants in a balanced fashion.

The problem with the display of patient information in the central frame was not immediately soluble, and the experiment was run in a pilot form with a group of 20 undergraduate students. By ensuring the only browser used was Netscape Navigator (with which the incremental writing trick worked reasonably well), and exhorting participants not to resize the experimental window, it was possible to use the system adequately to generate usable data. The experiment was reported by Yule, Cooper and Fox (1998).

Eventually a new interface was developed to overcome the limitations of the first, using dynamic HTML to change the appearance of the system radically. Instead of writing patient data to a separate window, a system of buttons was constructed, so that by clicking on a symptom button, the button itself would change to display the appropriate symptom information. A similar arrangement was used for diagnosis, and the whole was augmented by a few hidden feedback and help layers. An example of this interface is shown in Chapter 4 in the section on Dynamic HTML.

Initially the Dynamic HTML interface could not be used with Internet Explorer, owing to incompatibilities in the DHTML support among browsers. However, the relevant functionality was eventually added to make the system portable between the main browsers, and the system has been used in several experiments with variants of the medical diagnosis task. Published experiments (Cooper and Yule, 1999; Yule et al., 1998) have relied on groups of undergraduate students as participants, who performed the task on controlled machines on the departmental Intranet, but a number of student projects have made use of the Internet as a delivery system, allowing participants to access the experiment on their home computers or elsewhere and this seems to work quite reliably now.

The only major problem that has been encountered recently was caused by multiple clients trying to access the server at the same time. Normally web servers run many copies of the server in parallel, and each one services a different client, but this parallelism can cause problems when the different copies try to access the same datafiles at the same time, even to the extent of causing data loss. This problem has recently been solved by ensuring that all file-write operations merely append information to datafiles, so that nothing can be overwritten.

Case Study 3: Tandem Language Learning

C. Vogel

This section reports research in second-language acquisition that has taken advantage of the Internet for access to participants.[7] As with some of the psychological experiment clearing-houses described in Chapter 6, some of the work described here was not intended as a study relying on Internet access to participants, but rather had pedagogical requirements foremost in mind. At any rate, pedagogical utility first inspired the application family, and this has inspired subsequent research into its comparative efficacy.

One school of thought on second-language learning is that learner involvement in authentic texts and authentic communications is far more motivating (and hence productive) than certainly rote learning, but also learning in time with a structured syllabus. Any learning activity that engages the learner in autonomous (which does not imply unguided) study, especially raising learner awareness of the language itself, is deemed likely to have an overall positive effect on a speaker's second-language communicative abilities and accuracy.

One activity that has been common because of its success in raising linguistic awareness and inspiring learner autonomy is tandem language learning. In this model, pairs of learners meet to learn each other's language. Conversation proceeds (in the ideal) half of the time in each person's second language. Sometimes people think that this means that each speaker speaks in solely his or her native language, but this is far less efficacious than having each speaker produce and interpret both native language and second language. The native speakers are also encouraged to correct the non-native's second language, although it is acknowledged that neither partner is necessarily a competent grammar teacher. Nonetheless, the exercise is a good one for raising consciousness of the errors or awkwardnesses of style that one can make in first- and second-language production. The exercise is subject to risks as well, such as when language-learning partners become quite friendly towards each other, and their second-language learning reverts to secondary import-ance; however, this cannot really be deemed a negative failure of the activity (Appel and Mullen, 2000).

Little and Brammerts (1996) discuss an international project in elec-tronic tandem language learning.[8] Learners in 18 nations participate in the project, which identifies partners in appropriate language pairings and encourages tandem email exchanges.[9] Other Internet means of tandem learning, such as participations in MOOs, are also possible. Generally, collaborative tasks are suggested in order to move discussion beyond the introductions stage. The electronic forum for electronic communication forces a focus on writing (although there is a clear difference in register involved in many Internet-based communications and more formal forms of written composition), and this has been argued to bootstrap competence in formal registers.

The tandem email activity described by Little and Brammerts was set up specifically for Internet-based language learning; however it also immediately begs the question of whether it is successful, and that is where Internet research enters. Appel (1998) describes her research on seven pairs taking advantage of the Spanish/English tandem exchange. (Interestingly, some of the native Spanish speakers were participating via their undergraduate degree university in Denmark.) In her re-search, exchanges were restricted to email communication, rather than a synchronous (for example, MOO) situation. The basic idea is that asynchronous communication provides greater facilitation for reflection and development of awareness; however, no controlled studies that we know of yet verify this empirical prediction. Participants were given instructions on the principles of tandem language learning, as well as instructions on how to use email (where necessary).

> All students were asked to maintain contact with their partners for a minimum of a month, writing, if possible, two to three messages a week. They were all told that they would be requested to forward three messages of their choice to the Dublin coordinator by the end of the month. (Appel, 1998: 4)

That is, students were participating via their university-supplied email accounts, or, in the case of four participants based in Spain, through the single account controlled by their language teacher there.[10]

One of the main points of the study was an examination of post-participation interviews aimed at ascertaining what the participants gained from the exercise. Consciousness of the mistakes that one might make oneself in a second language, as informed by witnessing the second-language mistakes of one's partner, were quite common. In fact, a common theme was the report that correcting second-language mistakes of one's partner yielded greater insights than did the partner's native-language corrections of one's own second language. The asymmetry is certainly curious. Additionally, the submitted messages themselves revealed linguistic awareness.

Relevant to the current purposes of analysing Internet research methodology, the primary weakness of the study is in its reliance on participants to provide the researcher with copies of the email communications. The problem to the researcher is in not being able to compare the effectiveness of tandem email across participants on the basis of degree of involvement. The researcher is dependent on the participant's selection of emails to submit to the study. It could have happened that the participants who benefited the most were the ones who exchanged the most correspondence, and that would be the desired pedagogical outcome; however, under the research design employed, it is not possible fully to explore this issue. Essentially, the research requires a framework in which the researcher controls all of the data, without any doubts at all about the possibility of some messages having been neglected or lost for technical reasons.[11]

Appel and Mullen (1998) notice this problem. They note the following, quite in line with remarks made by Hewson et al. (1996) and throughout this book, in its emphasis on researcher control of the data.

> Research in this area has been impeded by a number of problems. The practical difficulties of arranging tandem correspondence programs, i.e. the pairing of international correspondents in experimental groups, have often proven to be more considerable than suspected. Difficulties in insuring accessibility of the necessary facilities, compatibility of various email applications across different platforms and standards, and the imperfectly solved problem of optimal methods of data collection have produced some confusion in the field of electronic tandem research. Some suggestions have been made as to the best way to go about email tandem exchanges, but other conclusions have proved in many cases more elusive due to the difficulty of controlled experimentation.

In response, Appel and Mullen provided an email server tailored to the tandem language learning needs. Their system is implemented in Perl and provides an email service with features constrained for the needs of tandem email communication. For example, participants can exchange correspondence with only their partners – thus, there is no distraction effect that might be accompanied by a fully functional free email service. As the server provides the communication facilities over the Web, the participants do not require individual email accounts at home, only Internet access. Moreover, it became possible to provide useful linguistic tools to provide automatic feedback to participants – a statistical language-guesser was incorporated to provide heuristic feedback to the participants on the relative amount of each language that their communications made use of (important given the tandem language learning paradigm emphasis on equal amounts of both languages). Additionally, there are links to online resources specific to language learner needs (but no facility for tracking user access to them).

The system is quite a nicely designed one for the purposes of conducting research on tandem email as a mode of second-language learning. It solves the problem of lack of researcher access to the entirety of the dataset involved in an experiment. However, it is clearly a case in which the researcher became designer and programmer in order to achieve a tailored system. The software in its published form was not available to other researchers (Appel and Mullen, 2000). For individuals who are interested in participating in the research as a member of a tandem partnership or as a teacher/researcher investigating learner communications, an extended version of the system reported by Appel and Mullen (2000) is available as a host server from *wilde.cs.tcd.ie:2222/f-tandem.html* (Christine Appel, personal communication). The system is a good example of topical research making crucial use of Internet facilities, and which has run into some of the same difficulties that we have emphasised here.

Lessons to be Learned

The case studies described above highlight several issues that can help guide researchers planning to implement Internet-mediated research. The main points, many of which restate issues raised earlier in the book, are summarised here. First, piloting of an Internet-mediated study is essential. All three studies outlined above encountered problems that could have been avoided by adopting alternative, more appropriate procedures. These problems included unanticipated behaviour of participants (study 1) and unanticipated behaviour of software (study 2). Clearly it is better to identify these issues during a pilot study phase. A second point illustrated in these studies is the trade-off between simple designs that do not require advanced programming skills, and more complex systems that enhance the study in various ways. In study 2, a more complex system was needed in order to achieve the features required in the experimental design, such as between-groups administration of materials. In case study 3 the initial implementation, which made use of email to allow study participants to interact, and then requested that they forward examples of this interaction to the researcher, was found to embody a lack of experimenter control that could threaten data validity. Consequently a more sophisticated system, developed in Perl, was produced that allowed many useful features to be incorporated. Case study 1, on the other hand, made use of a simple email-based methodology that was successful in fulfilling the research goals, though more sophisticated procedures could also have benefited this study (such as a method of participant tracking more reliable than recording email addresses). In study 1 a tendency for the Internet responses to be longer and more elaborate than the non-Internet responses was observed. This could be a general feature of IMR, but could also have been due to the effect of issue salience in this particular case. The advice we gave previously – to avoid posting to newsgroups without requesting permission from the administrator – is reinforced by study 1, which elicited a hostile response from one newsgroup moderator whose permission had not been sought prior to posting. Server overload, a problem that occurred in case study 2 above, was also noted earlier as a potential threat that could lead to data loss. In the above example, this problem was resolved via a modification that set the file-write process to append to rather than overwrite files.

The points highlighted above illustrate some of the issues raised throughout the book. The case studies reported here contrast in their approaches and the research questions addressed. Despite their shortcomings, they all demonstrate the potential of IMR for gathering valid and reliable data in social and behavioural research, given careful planning, design, and piloting.

Notes

1 Note that the groups contacted in this study were very likely to have an interest in the general research area (that is, the study had high issue salience, as discussed in Chapter 5). This willingness to participate in social or behavioural research may not generalise to non-academic populations accessed through the Internet, however, and issue salience is likely to be lower for these populations. Techniques that encourage participation should thus be implemented where possible (specific recommendations were given in Chapter 5).

2 Email replies containing responses were actually printed out and kept in hard copy format (this was the raw data). The response-coded data file was created by typing the data in by hand.

3 As already noted, high issue salience was a likely factor in encouraging responses. Further, this study was carried out in the relatively early days of the Internet, so there may also have been a novelty effect that encouraged participation.

4 As emphasised already, in previous chapters.

5 Having said this, the claims outlined in Chapter 3 about inherent biases in the characteristics of the Internet-user population may well have been more accurate at the time this study was carried out.

6 Further, statistical analysis can even be carried out automatically given a suitable interface.

7 Thanks are due to Christine Appel for useful discussion of methodology in applied linguistics generally, and the benefits and pitfalls of conducting IMR in applied

linguistics. This section outlines a programme of research that began with a pilot study conducted within her master's dissertation research.

8 Information about the project can be obtained from *www.slf.ruhr-uni-bochum.de/email/ idxeng00.html* or *www.tcd.ie/CLCS/tandem/*.

9 The countries are: Belgium, Canada, Denmark, France, Germany, Great Britain, Ireland, Italy, Japan, Korea, Netherlands, Peru, Portugal, Romania, Spain, Sweden, Turkey, and the USA.

10 Recall that this possibility was pointed out in Chapter 4, and the risks for data control elaborated in Chapter 6. The interaction of additional observation here (not just the researcher, but researcher and teacher) is hard to quantify. It is nearly impossible to assess the effect on language produced either in the native or second language by the fact that these participants' emails were processed by their teacher.

11 This discussion is not intended as a criticism of the findings of the study. It should be pointed out that this was among the first of its kind, and at a time when the proper methodological and technological issues in all dimensions of the research area were under discussion.

8

Conclusions

This book has outlined and discussed the issues that emerge in designing and implementing Internet-based research studies. It has also provided details of the range of instruments and procedures available to support Internet-mediated primary research, and has presented recommendations and guidelines aimed at allowing the practising researcher to construct well-planned, well-designed studies that use the Internet as a point of access to primary data. In addition, the book has outlined a range of resources available on the Internet that can support secondary research in the human sciences.

The resources available for secondary research were discussed in Chapter 2. The range of information available and the procedures needed to access this information were described, with an emphasis upon selecting those sources that are unlikely quickly to go out of date. Thus the aim was to provide the researcher or student with a knowledge of the resources available to support his or her research in the long term. The importance of assessing the quality of the information available on the Internet was also stressed, and recommendations given for ensuring that the sources used are reliable. Emphasis was also placed upon the use of techniques that maximise the efficiency and effectiveness of information retrieval.

Chapters 3, 4, and 5 focused on the use of the Internet as a tool for conducting primary research; that is, for gathering data from participants. Chapter 3 provided an introduction, highlighting a number of central theoretical and methodological issues that arise, including sampling bias, and levels of researcher control. The range of methodologies that can be supported in IMR were outlined, and the advantages and disadvantages of an IMR approach discussed. In Chapter 4 the possibilities raised in Chapter 3 were explored further, through an examination of the tools available, and the ways in which these can be used to gather data. A range of software technologies were described and explored, from fairly simple-to-use facilities, such as email and FTP, through to more complex Web-based technologies. Thus Chapter 4 provided an overview of the equipment available to support IMR, and the possibilities this enables. Chapter 5 provided more details on how to design and implement a Web-based survey. In Chapter 6 the problems that can arise in IMR were discussed and solutions offered. Some of these solutions directly addressed concerns raised in Chapter 3. The methodological issues addressed in Chapter 6 are relevant whether the researcher engages in direct involvement in the software technologies discussed in Chapter 4, or relies on one of the research study clearing-house systems described in Chapter 6. In Chapter 6 the way things can go wrong with IMR were classified into four main areas: equipment, methodology, netiquette, and security against hacking. Certain themes were common to all of these sections (ethics, proper control of materials, access to participants, and so on). And many issues were addressed here in a slightly different light than in which they appeared in Chapter 3 or Chapter 4. In short, we advocate maximal researcher control over materials and data. The case studies presented in Chapter 7 recapitulated many of the points raised throughout the book, and demonstrated the types of things that can go wrong in IMR, as well as offering ways of avoiding these pitfalls. Chapter 5 provided an introduction to the programming required to implement some of the procedures discussed in chapter 4, through a step-by-step description of how to develop a Web-based survey (though, as noted in Chapter 6, programming skills are not necessary in order to implement a WWW study, due to the design packages available).

The main conclusions of the book can be summarised in terms of the scope of Internet-mediated research, particularly in terms of the advantages it offers, and the problems that arise. We noted a number of advantages. First, the access to an extremely large and diverse pool of potential participants offers greater possibilities than ever before for conducting large-scale research, cross-cultural research, and accessing small populations. Second, access to participants is possible with increased cost- and time-efficiency. The benefits of this cannot be emphasised enough, especially for those researchers with more limited funding available for research. Research that would otherwise not be possible due to time or funding constraints can be conducted via the Internet. This is a feature that we expect will be particularly important for researchers and students at smaller institutions. The potential for automated data collection and analysis is another important feature of IMR, which also impacts upon its time- and cost-effectiveness. In an Internet study the data arrive in a format ready for analysis (that is, an electronic datafile), and this removes the need for an additional data-input phase. Further, if conducting a Web-based study, the administration of materials is automatic. Given a suitably sophisticated system, statistical analysis of data can also be automated. The consequent savings on both the time and cost of a piece of research can thus be substantial.

Some of the novel features of Internet-mediated communication were also highlighted as potential advantages of IMR. One feature noted was the possibility of maintaining complete anonymity whilst also allowing a degree of interactivity, which is not possible with more traditional methods. For example, in a chat room situation participants are able to disguise their true age, sex, nationality, and so on, and present themselves as they wish. This is also possible in an online interview situation. This opens up the potential for removing, or deliberately manipulating, biosocial attributes, and thus creates new possibilities in IMR not afforded in more traditional primary research contexts. This very same feature of Internet-based communication was raised earlier as a potential threat to data validity, since the researcher cannot be sure that participants are not providing misleading information about their personal characteristics. It is typically much easier to ascertain whether participants are truthfully reporting their sex, for example, in a traditional research context. We see no obvious way round this problem, other than to try to ascertain the extent of participant honesty through empirical studies that validate IMR procedures. The possibility of deliberately misleading participants about, for example, the researchers' sex, nationality, and so on, may be appealing for some types of research, but raises an ethical issue. While an individual researcher might be interested in the way participants respond differently to interviewers with different professed biosocial attributes (for example), deception may lead to participants disclosing personal information that they would not have done if they had known the researcher's true attributes. Debriefing participants about this deceit may then lead to anxiety, or anger. The extent to which researchers should feel comfortable about engaging in this type of deceit, from an ethical perspective, is unclear. This issue illustrates the way in which novel features of IMR can raise new ethical questions in social and behavioural research. The precise effects of researcher and participant characteristics in IMR remains to be explored.

A second feature of the Internet that we highlighted is that it provides an enormous body of readily available archived data, in the form of logs of online communications, published articles, and so on, which can be used as primary data in social and behavioural research. Linguistic observation and discourse analytic studies are those that may obviously benefit here. The availability of records of online interactions increases the scope for conducting unobtrusive observational research, which can be far more problematic in traditional research contexts. Further possible advantages of IMR have been speculated about, such as increased candidness, higher response rates, and reduction of experimental demand characteristics. The effects of particular Internet research methodologies on these factors is not yet clear, and requires further research.

Throughout the book we have highlighted problems that may arise in IMR, though we see these not so much as disadvantages, but more as pitfalls that may emerge if preventative measures are not taken. In Chapter 6 we provided solutions for pre-empting and recovering from potential problems. Two major issues that emerge as possible threats to data validity in IMR are sampling bias and levels of researcher control. The issue of sampling was addressed at length in Chapter 3, and we concluded that sampling bias does not pose a particular problem for Internet-mediated research. We assessed the popular claim that the Internet-user population is itself a highly skewed sample of the population at large, by considering the evidence on which this claim is based. This evidence comes from Internet-user surveys, which we noted cannot accurately represent the entire Internet-user population, due to the sampling procedures employed. We then examined data concerning Internet composition (that is, availability of Internet access world-wide) as an alternative source of evidence and argued that this evidence indicates the vastness and diversity of the Internet-user population. Further, we noted that in traditional research reliance on small homogenous samples is common, and that in this context IMR can open up possibilities for accessing more diverse samples than have typically been readily available. Another point noted was that broad generalisability is not always required, and one of the major advantages of IMR is the potential for targeting, and accessing larger samples from special populations.

Taking all the above considerations into account, we do not consider inherent biases in the Internet-user population a problem for IMR. However, we do emphasise that the sampling methodologies employed will influence the types of samples obtained, and thus these methodologies need to be carefully selected in relation to the research goals. Indeed, we are concerned about the current reliance on volunteer participants in IMR, due to the biases this may introduce, especially when a large number of studies seem to place their participation advertisements in locations most likely to attract those interested in the particular research topic, or in IMR itself. In sum, we argue that if sampling procedures are carefully selected (we outline a number of possibilities), data validity will not be compromised. This includes placing advertisements for participation strategically if recruiting volunteers, and considering alternatives where practicable, and where the research question is more likely to be affected by the use of volunteer participants. The effects of using different sampling methodologies in IMR needs to be researched.

A second major issue in IMR, which is a potential threat to data validity, and which has been discussed at length throughout this book, relates to levels of researcher control. There are particular features of IMR that can lead to reduced levels of researcher control (over materials, procedures and data) compared with traditional research methods. First, it is more difficult for the researcher to verify that information provided by the participant is accurate. This issue was raised in relation to informed consent. Given the indirect, non-proximal nature of Internet interactions, there is more scope for participants to deceive the researcher about factors such as their age, sex, nationality, and so on. We doubt that such deception is likely to be widespread, but for studies that do rely on the accuracy of such information (for example, studies looking at gender differences), it is recommended to take measures to compare results with a non-Internet sample (where the accuracy of relevant information can be verified). A second issue concerns the lack of control over the participation conditions. Variations may occur in IMR that are more easily controllable and measurable in traditional research methodologies (for example, distractions present, level of intoxication, time of day). The effects of such factors in IMR need researching. A third potential problem is software and hardware variation. Different participants will most likely be using different platforms and interfaces, which can result in variations in the way materials appear, the speed at which events occur, and so on. This issue has been discussed extensively throughout this book, and various solutions for maximising control have been offered. It is ultimately up to the individual researcher to decide which solution can best address this issue in his or her own research. For example, one suggestion we made was to restrict study participation to an Intranet environment; this may be appropriate for some research questions but not others. Another possibility is to use technologies that are less likely to give rise to variations, such as simple text-based email administrations. Again, the feasibility of this solution will depend upon the particular research question. In sum, we noted that there is often a trade-off between developing materials and procedures that are ideally suited to the research question, and adopting methodologies that allow adequate levels of control over the materials and procedures used.

To summarise the above points, we have outlined some very attractive features of Internet-mediated research, and highlighted the ways in which it can enhance, as well as open up new possibilities for, primary research. While potential problems have been outlined, workable solutions have also been offered. As the technologies currently available develop, and research into IMR expands, further solutions will become available. We have noted the potential for IMR to support a range of methodologies, including surveys, interviews, observational studies, and experiments. An obvious limitation of IMR, regardless of emerging technologies, is that it cannot be used to implement any study that requires direct proximal interaction (though developments in video and sound technologies may certainly narrow the distinction between Internet and non-Internet interaction in this respect). Overall, however, we consider the advantages and possibilities in Internet-mediated primary research to far outweigh the problems and limitations.

So what is the current state of Internet-mediated research? Many issues are just beginning to be addressed, and solutions offered. A main aim of this book has been to explore these issues and offer our own solutions. The clear trend is that more and more researchers are coming to acknowledge the potential of the Internet to enhance their own research. However, many of the studies that are appearing online seem to suffer from many of the features we warn against (though we are not necessarily saying they have not produced useful results). For example, most studies make use of volunteer participants, often recruited by advertising primarily on Internet research-related sites, or by posting to newsgroups related to the research topic. Many studies do not appear to implement procedures to ensure ethical standards (such as obtaining informed consent, or making it easy to withdraw from the study at any time). Many studies are poorly designed, in that instructions are ambiguous, download times are long, and materials are not clearly presented. Such weaknesses may arise due to the lack of a set of clear, comprehensive guidelines for conducting Internet-mediated primary research. We hope that this book has made some headway in developing such guidelines. Indeed, many of the criticisms just outlined have applied directly to our own attempts to conduct Internet-based research studies (see the discussion of case studies in Chapter 7). However, another factor that may account for poorly implemented Internet-mediated studies is the failure to apply the same rigorous design process as in more traditional methodologies, due to an overemphasis on the Internet as a means of gathering large volumes of data at great speed. While we have also pointed out the potential of IMR for accessing large, diverse samples quickly, we cannot emphasise enough the importance of rigorous planning and piloting of procedures. This is essential in ensuring data validity. Given careful design and planning, however, we consider the scope of Internet-mediated research to be vast, especially in the context of the continuing rapid growth of the Internet.

Our final advice to the researcher who wants to implement an Internet-based study is to engage in thorough planning and piloting, with reference to the issues raised throughout this book. A variety of tools and procedures are available, and these must be chosen in accord with the particular research goals. While we believe that Internet-mediated primary research has great potential, it is still in its infancy. The technologies and procedures available need researching further. We encourage practising researchers to make use of IMR in their own research, where appropriate, and we urge further exploration and validation of the procedures available. In particular, we encourage researchers from disciplines other than those we focus our examples on (our focus having been primarily on psychology, linguistics, and cognitive science) to apply, and if necessary adapt, the procedures we have outlined to their own research domains.

The way for IMR to evolve is for researchers to implement procedures, identify problems that emerge, and seek solutions. The guidelines we have developed in this book have been influenced by our own implementations of Internet-mediated primary research. While these guidelines may be the most comprehensive to date, we certainly do not claim to have covered all the pitfalls that can arise, or to have provided the best solutions to address the problems recognised. The scope of IMR remains to be explored in many new areas and applications.

References

Appel, M.C. (1998). The development of language awareness and learner autonomy in tandem language learning via e-mail. In *Proceedings XVI Congreso Nacional de AESLA*. Universidad de La Rioja, 22–5 April.

Appel, M.C. and Mullen, T. (1998). A common gateway interface for tandem language learning. In B. Strotmann (ed.), *Proceedings of the International Congress on Technology in Teaching*. IATEFL Computer SIG, TESOL Spain, Universidad Europea de Madrid, 20–2 November.

Appel, M.C. and Mullen, T. (2000). Pedagogical considerations for Web-based tandem language exchange. *Computers and Education*, 34(3–4), 291–308.

Berzsenyi, C.A. (1999). Chat theory: Renovating rhetorical education in electronic composition classrooms. In *The Penn State Conference on Rhetoric and Composition Rhetorical Education in America*, 4–7 July. *www.wb.psu.edu/faculty/berzsenyi/ cbpres.html*.

Birnbaum, M. (2001) *Introduction to Behavioral Research on the Internet*. Upper Saddle River, NJ: Prentice-Hall.

Bogaert, A.F. (1996). Volunteer bias in human sexuality research: evidence for both sexuality and personality differences in males. *Archives of Sexual Behaviour*, 25(2), 125–40.

Bordia, P. (1996). Studying verbal interaction on the Internet: the case of rumor transmission research. *Behaviour Research Methods, Instruments and Computers*, 28(2), 149–51.

Bradley, N. (1999). Sampling for Internet surveys: an examination of respondent selection for Internet research. *Journal of the Market Research Society*, 41(4), 387–95.

Browndyke, J.N., Santa Maria, M.P., Pinkston, J. and Gouvier, W. (1998). A survey of general head injury and prevention knowledge between professionals and non-professionals. *www.premier.net/%7Ecogito/project/onp1_poster.html*.

Buchanan, T. (2000). Internet research: Self-monitoring and judgments of attractiveness. *Behavior Research Methods, Instruments and Computers*, 32, 521–27.

Buchanan, T. and Smith, J.L. (1999a). Using the Internet for psychological research: personality testing on the World Wide Web. *British Journal of Psychology*, 90, 125–44.

Buchanan, T. and Smith, J.L. (1999b). Research on the Internet: validation of the World-Wide Web mediated personality scale. *Behavior Research Methods, Instruments and Computers*, 31, 565–71.

Coomber, R. (1997a). Using the Internet for survey research. *Sociological Research Online*, 2(2). *www.socresonline.org.uk/socresonline/2/2/html*.

Coomber, R. (1997b). Dangerous drug adulteration – an international survey of drug dealers using the Internet and World Wide Web (WWW). *International Journal of Drug Policy*, 8(2), 71–81.

Cooper, R. and Yule, P. (1999). Comparative modelling of learning in a decision making task. *Proceedings of the 21st Annual Conference of the Cognitive Science Society*, Vancouver, BC.

Couper, P. (2000). Web surveys: a review of issues and approaches. *Public Opinion Quarterly*, 64(4), 464–94.

Coye, R.W. (1985). Characteristics of participants and non-participants in experimental research. *Psychological Reports*, 56(1), 19–25. Dissertation. *www.cs.tcd.ie/courses/ csll/ kenny98.ps.gz*.

Dahlen, M. (1998). Controlling the uncontrollable: toward the perfect Web sample. Paper presented at the *ESOMAR Worldwide Internet Seminar and Exhibition*, 28–30 January, Paris.

Davis, R.N. (1999). Web-based administration of a personality questionnaire: comparison with traditional methods. *Behaviour Research Methods, Instruments and Computers*, 31(4), 572–7.

Dobrzynski, J.H. (2000). Cyberauctions try to stop shill bidding: Ebay watches for players who form rings to artificially raise prices. *International Herald Tribune*, 3–4 June.

Dollinger, S.J. and Frederick, T. (1993). Volunteer bias and the five-factor model. *Journal of Psychology*, 127(1), 29–36.

Double, R. (1985). The case against the case against belief. *Mind*, 375, 420–30.

Fox, J. (1980). Making decisions under the influence of memory. *Psychological Review*, 87, 190–211.

Fox, R., Crask, M.R. and Kim, J. (1988). Mail survey response rates: a meta-analysis of selected techniques for inducing response. *Public Opinion Quarterly*, 52(4), 467–91.

Gangstead, S.W. and Snyder, M. (1985). 'To carve nature at its joints': on the existence of discrete classes in personality. *Psychological Review*, 92, 317–40.

Goeritz, A.S. and Schumacher, J. (2000). The WWW as a research medium: an illustrative survey on paranormal belief. *Perceptual & Motor Skills*, 90, 1195–1206.

Goyder, J.C. (1982). Further evidence on factors affecting response rates to mailed questionnaires. *American Sociological Review*, 47(4), 550–3.

Griffiths, M.D. (1999). Internet addiction: fact or fiction? *The Psychologist*, 12(5), 246–50.

Guennouni, M. (2000). Extension of a Web-based environment for cognitive science experiments. Department of Computer Science, Trinity College, University of Dublin. Moderatorship in Computer Science, Linguistics and French. Final project dissertation.

GVU (1997). Graphics Visualisation and Usability Center 7th WWW user survey. *www.gvu.gatech.edu/user_surveys/survey-1997-04*. Georgia Tech Research Corporation, Atlanta, GA.

Healey, P. (1995). Communication as a special case of misunderstanding: semantic coordination in dialogue. PhD. thesis, Centre for Cognitive Science, University of Edinburgh.

Heberlein, T.A. and Baumgartner, R. (1978). Factors affecting response rates to mailed questionnaires: a quantitative analysis of the published literature. *American Sociological Review*, 43(4), 447–62.

Herring, S.C. (1996). Posting in a different voice: gender and ethics in computer-mediated communication. In C. Ess (ed.), *Philosophical Perspectives in Computer Mediated Communication*. New York: State University of New York Press.

Herring, S.C., Johnson, D.A. and DiBenedetto, T. (1998). Participation in electronic discourse in a 'feminist' field. In J. Coates (ed.), *Language and Gender: A Reader*. Oxford: Blackwell.

Hewson, C.M. (1994). Empirical evidence regarding the folk psychological concept of belief. In A. Ram and K. Eiselt (eds), *Proceedings of the Sixteenth Annual Conference of the Cognitive Science Society*, Altanta, GA.

Hewson, C.M. and Vogel, C.M. (1994). Psychological evidence for assumptions of path-based inheritance reasoning. In A. Ram and K. Eiselt (eds), *Proceedings of the Sixteenth Annual Conference of the Cognitive Science Society*, Altanta, GA.

Hewson, C.M., Laurent, D. and Vogel, C. (1996). Proper methodologies for psychological and sociological experiments administered via Internet. *Behavior Research Methods, Instruments and Computers*, 28(2), 186–91.

Jones, R.A. (1994). The ethics of research in cyberspace. *Internet Research*, 4(3). *www.emerald-library.com/brev/17204cc1.htm*.

Kalton, G. and Schuman, H. (1982). The effect of the question on survey responses: a review. *Journal of the Royal Statistical Society*, 145, part 1, 42–73.

Kanuk, L. and Berenson, C. (1975). Mail surveys and response rates: a literature review. *Journal of Marketing Research*, XII, 440–53.

Kaye, B.K. and Johnson, T.J. (1999). Research methodology: taming the cyber frontier. *Social Science Computer Review*. Thousand Oaks, 17(3), 323–37. Sage Publications Inc. (accessed online @ Proquest).

Keller, F., Corley, M., Corley, S., Konieczny, L. and Todirascu, A. (1998). Webexp: a Java toolbox for Web-based psychological experiments. Tech. Rep. HCRC/TR-99, University of Edinburgh.

Kennedy, A.J. (2001). *The Rough Guide to the Internet 2001*. Harmondsworth: Penguin.

Kenny, S. (1998). A generic automatic experiment creation and presentation tool. Department of Computer Science, Trinity College, University of Dublin. Moderatorship in Computer Science, Linguistics and French. Final project.

Kent, P. (2001). *The Complete Idiot's Guide to the Internet*, 7th edition. Que.

Kiesler, S. and Sproull, L. (1986). Response effects in the electronic survey. *Public Opinion Quarterly*, 50, 402–13.

Kiesler, S., Siegel, J. and McGuire, T.W. (1984). Social psychological aspects of computer-mediated communication. *American Psychologist*, 39(10), 1123–34.

Krantz, J.H., Ballard, J. and Scher, J. (1997). Comparing the results of laboratory and World Wide Web samples of the determinants of female attractiveness. *Behaviour Research Methods, Instruments and Computers*, 29, 264–9.

Landweber, L. (1997) International connectivity, version 16, 15 June. *ftp://ftp.cs.wisc.edu/connectivity_table/version_16.text*.

Lehnert, W.G. (1998). *Internet 101: A Beginner's Guide to the Internet and the World Wide Web*. Addison Wesley.

Little, D. and Brammerts, H. (1996). A guide to language learning in tandem via the Internet. Tech. Rep. 46, Centre for Language and Communication Studies, Trinity College, University of Dublin. CLCS Occasional Paper.

Lottor, M. (1992). Internet growth (1981–1991). Network Working Group, Request for Comments: 1296. Anonymous ftp from *nic.merit.edu, file documents/rfc/rfc1296.txt*.

Lottor, M. (1996). Internet Domain Survey: January 1996. *www.nw.com*.

McGowan, C. (1999). Extension of a web based environment for cognitive science experiments, with testing for metaphor. Department of Computer Science, Trinity College, University of Dublin. Moderatorship in Computer Science, Linguistics and French. Final project dissertation.

McGraw, K. and Tew, M. (1997). Psychology experiments on the Internet: use of Shockwave technology. *home.olemiss.edu/~pymcgraw/fipse.htm*.

McNemar, Q. (1946). Opinion-attitude methodology. *Psychological Bulletin*, 43, 289–374.

Mann, C. and Stewart, F. (2000). *Internet Communication and Qualitative Research: A Handbook for Researching Online*. London: Sage.

Martin, C.L. (1994). The impact of topic interest on mail survey response behaviour. *Journal of the Market Research Society*, 36(4), 327–37.

Mehta, R. and Sivadas, E. (1995). Comparing response rates and response content in mail versus electronic mail surveys. *Journal of the Market Research Society*, 37(4), 428–39.

MIDS (1998). Matrix Information and Directory Services (MIDS). *www.mids.org*.

Morokoff, P.J. (1986). Volunteer bias in the psychophysiological study of female sexuality. *Journal of Sex Research*, 22(1), 19–25.

Murphy, P.R., Daley, J. and Dalenberg, D.R. (1991). Exploring the effects of postcard prenotification on industrial firms' response to mail surveys. *Journal of the Market Research Society*, 33(4), 335–45.

O'Dochartaigh (2001). *The Internet Research Handbook: A Practical Guide for Students and Researchers in the Social Sciences*. London: Sage.

Parallax (1996). Parallax Web Design: Internet facts. *www.parallaxweb.com/interfacts.html*.

Penkoff, D.W., Colman, R.W. and Katzman, S.L. (1996). From paper-and-pencil to screen-and-keyboard: toward a methodology for survey research on the Internet. Paper presented at the Annual Conference of the International Communication Association, May, Chicago.

Pincott, G. and Braithwaite, A. (2000). Nothing new under the sun? *International Journal of Market Research*, 42(2), 137–55.

Pitcow, J.E. and Recker, M.M. (1994) Results from the first World Wide Web User Survey. *www.cc.gatech.edu/gvu/user_surveys/survey-01-1994/survey-paper.html*.

Rossetti, P. (1998). Gender differences in e-mail communication. *The Internet TESL Journal*, IV(7). *www.aitech.ac.jp/,iteslj/Articles/RossettiGenderDif.html*.

Ryan, N. (2001). *Web based experimentation in cognitive science*, Department of Computer Science, Trinity College, University of Dublin. Moderatorship in computer science, linguistics and French. Final project Dissertation.

Schillewaert, N., Langerak, F. and Duhamel, T. (1998). Non-probability sampling for WWW surveys: a comparison of methods. *Journal of the Market Research Society*, 40(4), 307–22.

Schmidt, W.C. (1997). World Wide Web survey research: benefits, potential problems, and solutions. *Behaviour Research Methods, Instruments and Computers*, 29, 270–3.

Schütze, C. (1996). *The Empirical Base of Linguistics: Grammaticality Judgements and Linguistic Methodology*. Chicago: University of Chicago Press.

Sell, R.L. (1997). Research and the Internet: an e-mail survey of sexual orientation. *American Journal of Public Health*, 87, 297.

Senior, C. and Smith, M. (1999). The Internet: a possible research tool. *Psychologist*, 12(9), 442–5.

Senior, C., Barnes, J., Jenkins, R., Landau, S., Phillips, M.L. and David, A.S. (1999). Attribution of social dominance and maleness to schematic faces. *Social Behaviour and Personality*, 27(4), 331–8.

Sheehan, K.B. and McMillan, S.J. (1999). Response variation in e-mail surveys: an exploration. *Journal of Advertising Research*, 39(4), 45–54.

Smart, R. (1966). Subject selection bias in psychological research. *Canadian Psychologist*, 7, 115–21.

Smith, C.B. (1997). Casting the Net: surveying an Internet population. *Journal of Computer Mediated Communication*, 3,(1).Online: *jcmc.huji.ac.il/vol3/issue1/smith.html* accessed 29/4/02.

Smith, H.W. (1975). *Strategies of Social Research: The Methodological Imagination*. London: Prentice Hall.

Smith, J.A., Harré, R. and Langenhove, L.K. (1995). *Rethinking Methods in Psychology*. London: Sage.

Smith, M.A. and Leigh, B. (1997). Virtual subjects: using the Internet as an alternative source of subjects and research environment. *Behaviour, Research Methods, Instruments and Computers*, 29(4), 496–505.

Stanton, J.M. (1998). An empirical assessment of data collection using the Internet. *Personnel Psychology*, 51(3), 709–25.

Stich, S. (1983). *From Folk Psychology to Cognitive Science: The Case Against Belief*. Cambridge, MA: Bradford Books/MIT Press.

Stones, A. and Perry, D. (1997). Survey questionnaire data on panic attacks gathered using the World-Wide Web. *Depression and Anxiety*, 6, 86–7.

Strassberg, D.S. and Kristi, L. (1995). Volunteer bias in sexuality research. *Archives of Sexual Behaviour*, 24(4), 369–82.

Strauss, J. (1996). Early survey research on the Internet: review, illustration and evaluation. In E.A. Blair and W.A. Kamakura (eds), *Proceedings of the American Marketing Association Winter Educators' Conference*. Chicago: American Marketing Association.

Sudman, S. (1980). Reducing response error in surveys. *The Statistician*, 29(4), 237–73.

Swoboda, W.J., Muhlberger, N., Weitkunat, R. and Schneeweib, S. (1997). Internet surveys by direct mailing. *Social Science Computer Review*, 15, 242–55.

Szabo, A. and Frenkl, M.D. (1996). Consideration of research on the Internet: guidelines and implications for human movement studies. *Clinical Kinesiology*, 50(3), 58–65.

Szabo, A., Frenkl, R. and Caputo, A. (1996). Deprivation feelings, anxiety, and commitment to various forms of physical activity: a cross-sectional study on the Internet. *Psychologia*, 39, 223–30.

Taylor, S. and Lynn, P. (1998). The effect of a preliminary notification letter on response to a postal survey of young people. *Journal of the Market Research Society*, 40(2), 165–78.

Timothy, B. (2000). Using a web-based tool for conducting cognitive science experiments. Department of Computer Science, Trinity College, University of Dublin. Moderatorship in Computer Science, Linguistics and French. Final project dissertation.

Tse, A.C.B. (1998). Comparing the response rate, response speed and response quality of two methods of sending questionnaires: e-mail versus mail. *Journal of the Market Research Society*, 40(4), 353–61.

Tse, A.C.B., Tse, K.C., Yin, C.H., Ting, C.B., Yi, K.W., Yee, K.P. and Hong, W.C. (1995). Comparing two methods of sending out questionnaires: e-mail versus mail. *Journal of the Market Research Society*, 37(4), 441–6.

Wason, P.C. and Johnson-Laird, P.N. (1972). *Psychology of Reasoning: Structure and Content.* Cambridge, MA: Harvard University Press.

Witmer, D.F., Colman, R.W. and Katzman, S.L. (1999). From paper-and-pencil to screen-and-keyboard. In S. Jones (ed.), *Doing Internet Research*. London: Sage.

Yammarino, F.J., Skinner, S. and Childers, T.L. (1991). Understanding mail survey response behaviour. *Public Opinion Quarterly*, 55(4), 613–39.

Yule, P., Cooper, R. and Fox, J. (1998). Normative and information processing accounts of medical diagnosis. *Proceedings of the 20th Annual Conference of the Cognitive Science Society.* Madison, WI.

Zakon, R.H. (2000). Hobbes' Internet timeline v.5.0. *www.isoc.org/zakon/ Internet/History/ HIT.html.*

Index